The Modern Secretary's Complete Guide

The Modern Secretary's Complete Guide

Twyla K. Schwieger

Parker Publishing Company, Inc.
West Nyack, N. Y.

Second Printing . . . . February, 1977

PRINTED IN THE UNITED STATES OF AMERICA
ISBN-0-13-597591-3
B & P

How This Book Will Help You

This book reaches the core of secretarial duties. It tells you how your work can be done, it shows you how your work can be done; it belongs at your side for ready reference as you do your work.

A host of illustrations are included in the book. They range from specialized mini notes to reports.

The material in this book has a flexibility that will allow you to adapt material in its entirety or combine the material presented here with your own ideas and suggestions to meet your office needs.

This unique approach to the office workload will enable you to control the work flow, and will dissolve your secretarial chores into secretarial achievements as you perform with enthusiasm and pride.

The proposed systems described in this book are to help you handle each office task from beginning to the point of completeness.

If your *job* depends on your *work,* this book should provide you with a good foundation for your secretarial career.

This book will help you perform your duties quickly and confidently when you are left alone in the office.

It will prompt you to evaluate your office needs and encourage you to develop a system that will make your office productive and orderly.

More specifically, this book offers to assist you by:

- softening new-job bewilderment as it relates to office atmosphere, office traffic, and business activity.

• providing you with hints and visual aids for becoming a poised business hostess. A simple and easy guide to proper introductions is included. Tips on scheduling appointments, keeping your boss on schedule, and canceling appointments are included.

• eliminating the exclamation mark when relaying a telephone call. You need not make this delayed announcement: "Oh! Mr. Doe called while you were out to lunch." There are suggestions on what to do with recorded telephone calls and office visits.

• passing on to you suggestions for keeping the mail current; how to process the mail, how to cut dictation time, and how to save your boss hours of reading time. Included are pointers for tracing traveling office mail.

• presenting to you ideas to put to use during dictation sessions. Utilize the spans of time during a dictation sitting to identify rush letters, make carbon copy notations, insert punctuation marks, and build your vocabulary. There is a brief discussion on writing implements.

• outlining for you the key to attractively typed letters; correct placement of the parts of a business letter; pointers for selecting the letter style. Models of the written address and salutation for academic, business, ecclesiastical, governmental, and professional positions are listed.

• sharing with you information about carbon copy notations, penned postscript notations, enclosure notations, mailing instructions, and a notation for a personally delivered letter.

• passing on to you mailing tips that are real office helpers.

• making it possible for you to breeze through a concise chapter on punctuation, spelling, capitalization, abbreviations, titles, and numbers.

• disclosing tips on erasing at the typewriter, race-with-time typing assignments, centering typing projects, headings and tables, use of the tabulator—save calculating time and typing time on columns of figures and financial reports.

• revealing to you office shortcuts—a new approach to entire-word corrections, a simple way to find the center of various widths and lengths of paper; how to extend the office life of rubber stamps; how to race the clock by using a new envelope stuffing technique.

● introducing the Executive Reminder Note; how to strengthen your secretarial ability as it relates to your follow-up responsibility—reminder notes, calendars, cards, and folders.

● approaching the office duty of filing with renewed interest. In Chapter 14, four filing systems—alphabetical, numerical, geographic, and subject—are illustrated. Eliminate reshuffling of file folders and filing cabinet drawer labels by using the suggested file drawer capacity guide. Prepare your file folders for durability and neatness. Promote faster filing, finding, and quick identification with color.

● supplying you with business meeting aids such as the membership list and attendance record, preliminary preparations, and what to do following the meetings.

● furnishing you with helpful hints that will make planning the business trip easier. (Must you assemble publicity packets prior to business trips?) Chapter 16 covers material to be considered before typing the itinerary such as the preferred time of day for traveling, surface transportation; hotel reservations. Illustrated in this chapter is a special form designed for the travel folder.

● relinquishing to you the special services that your boss will appreciate; when to type mini notes for him; how to type the letters that lean to the social side of his busy schedule. (Keep records for him as you prepare remittances for his personal bills.)

You will find information on ordering stationery and supplies; how to utilize your leisure time for the benefit of yourself and your employer.

Until the time comes when you train your successor following the step-by-step procedure, you may make the "best-groomed and most gracious lady" list by reviewing the chapter on etiquette, office manners, and how to dress appropriately for your position in the office.

All this will help you attain the respected status of a first-rate secretary.

Twyla K. Schwieger

ACKNOWLEDGMENTS

Acknowledgment is made to the following:

for providing information quoted in the manuscript:

> C. K. Collins, Assistant Vice President, American Telephone and Telegraph Company, New York;
>
> Milton O. Fletcher, Manager, Chamber of Commerce of the United States, Washington, D.C.;
>
> Post Office Department, Washington, D.C.;
>
> Customer Relations Branch, United States Post Office, Denver, Colorado.

for supplying material for use in the manuscript:

> G. L. Anneler, Manager, Teller Section (at the time material was supplied for the manuscript), United Bank of Denver, N.A., Denver, Colorado;
>
> William B. Cox, Special Representative, The Atchison, Topeka and Santa Fe Railway Company, Topeka, Kansas;
>
> Leonard Holmstrom, Passenger Traffic Manager, Northern Pacific Railway Company, St. Paul, Minnesota;
>
> Mrs. Elizabeth Denham, Secretariat Staff, Department of State (Protocol), Washington, D.C.;
>
> Mrs. Betty Mayer, Secretary to R. H. Shepler, Secretary of the Board and Senior Vice President, United Bank of Denver, N.A., Denver, Colorado.

for written permission to use material illustrated in the manuscript:

> Delbert L. James, Vice President and Cashier, First National Bank of Kansas City, Kansas City, Missouri;
>
> J. R. Andrews, Secretary-Treasurer, Woehrmyer Printing Co., Denver, Colorado;
>
> William K. Ryan, Vice President/Advertising, Wilson Jones Company, Chicago, Illinois;
>
> Barbara Rice, Secretary to John D. Devaney, Director-Legal Proceedings, United Air Lines, Chicago, Illinois;
>
> Ernest J. Portenstein, Executive Assistant Manager (for Hernando Courtright), Beverly Wilshire Hotel, Beverly Hills, California;
>
> Daisy Weichel, Director of Public Relations, The Boston Statler-Hilton, Boston, Massachusetts;
>
> Marion Swannie, Manager, Design Program Coordination, International Business Machines Corporation, New York;

9

R. B. Johnson, Passenger Traffic Manager, Union Pacific Railroad
Company, Omaha, Nebraska.

for supplying information, material, and for reviewing the itinerary for the manuscript:

David N. Brictson, Attorney, Frontier Airlines, Denver, Colorado.

for verbal assistance in the preparation of the manuscript:

John Hulse, General Commercial and Marketing Manager (Nebraska
area), Northwestern Bell Telephone Company, Omaha, Nebraska.

Appreciation is here expressed to the many persons who opened the
channels of communication with those individuals who actually supplied the
information and illustrations for the manuscript; particularly, Mrs. Charlotte
Snyder, Public Relations Officer, United Bank of Denver, N.A. Denver,
Colorado.

A special "thank you" is due Marie Rennecker, Professor Emeritus;
formerly Head of the English Department, Nebraska Western College,
Scottsbluff, Nebraska, for her helpful discussion and suggestions during the
preparation of the manuscript.

A special "thank you" is due Edith Thompson Hall, Lincoln Nebraska,
for her assistance throughout the preparation of the manuscript.

I owe thanks to my husband for his encouragement and help.

Twyla K. Schwieger

Contents

List of Illustrations

The Modern Secretary's Complete Guide

1

Orienting Yourself to a New Position

The following tips should help smooth your transfer from one office or organization to another.

Although one of the most noticeable adjustments may be your having to establish rapport with the personalities that will surround you, suggestions for smoothing your office move relate primarily to your work performance, rather than the get-acquainted phase of the office.

Listen to what is being said about each of your responsibilities. This deserves undivided attention from you. If you don't understand a procedure, ask questions. One employer said he would prefer to be "asked a thousand questions than to have a new employee make a mistake." If you think through the various stages of work as they have been presented to you, you probably will have fewer than a thousand questions and your questions may indicate that you have absorbed some of the facts pointed out to you during the training period.

When several steps are involved in a transaction, jot them down on paper. Concentrate on the material that is being explained to you; concentration may be more helpful to you than if you try to write down the instructions word for word.

The Spoken Address.   It is important to point out here that you be aware of how individuals within the office are addressed. Formality requirements may differ among offices. Don't rely solely on the informality that may have taken place during the interview. When you become a part of the office scene, listen to clues relating to the degree of formality or informality which you may exercise. You may be able to judge by an introduction as to the use of one's first name or last name. Some individuals to whom you are introduced may ask that you address them by their first names. If in doubt as to how you should address fellow workers, use a gender title and the surname (Mr. Barker, Mrs. Adams, or Miss Evans).

Public Relations.   Your organization may provide services for its customers whereby any one of the employees is expected to accommodate the customer efficiently. This arrangement may indicate that the customer is valued as a purchaser and friend, and that no employee is scolded for his willingness to serve everyone. With this procedure, every employee, titled or not, may be expected to greet the customers immediately. You may be expected to serve customers either through direct service or by directing or escorting them to the individual or department that can give them the service that they are seeking.

At times you may be requested by your supervisor or other authorized co-worker to *compile* detailed information that is to be released to an office visitor, but, because of the organization's policy, only your supervisor or another designated person is to *release* the information to the office visitor.

The Workload Preview.   During your training period, ask for a verbal summary of the most recent events and projects undertaken by the organization. Ask, also, for a briefing on the most important future events and projects of the company and how they will involve your particular office or job. You will then have an idea of how active your visitor list and meeting schedule might be in the future.

If you are not familiar with the purpose of the organization or the product or service of the company, ask for background material—pamphlets, brochures, advertising material, or any other material that will help to acquaint you with the work you do.

Read the bylaws of the organization, if a copy is available to you. Search for established meeting dates and prepare for these events, although the meetings may be months away. Check your calendars. If a notation of the various scheduled meetings does not appear on your calendars, make a notation for each meeting.

Printed material may provide other necessary information for you such as names which you should recognize through telephone calls and correspondence, social gatherings arranged by the company, and special meetings which include individuals not on the employee list but who have an interest in the organization.

2

The Business Hostess

You are the business office hostess, and the public relations phase is highlighted here. You represent your boss in his absence and you represent the company. Visitors form their opinions by your courtesy and efficiency.

If the company has any promotional material, have a rack for displaying this material. Or have some other reading material available, to bridge the time gap when your boss cannot see the visitor immediately upon arrival. (If you have some reading material available for visitors, they may not be so prone to scan your desk top.)

When the visitor arrives, it is your responsibility to greet him and to identify yourself, if he has a confirmed appointment and if you have communicated with him prior to his visit to your office.

Chairs, of course, will always be available, but some people will wait for an invitation to be seated. Invite the visitors to be seated, provide ash trays; and keep an extra book of matches in your desk drawer for the visitor who wants to smoke but has no matches.

The Visitor Comes to You. Many companies supply their representatives with business calling cards. The visitor usually presents the business calling card to you as he approaches your desk. Before you announce to your boss that the visitor has arrived, be sure that you know the exact pronunciation of the visitor's name.

If the visitor does not have a business calling card, write his name and the name of the firm he represents, and any other pertinent information, such as his title, on a small piece of paper. Present this in the same manner as you would a printed card.

Forms often save time. If a do-it-yourself project is worth the time, supplies, and effort, you may want to have a few simple cards ready for this purpose. Type the information lines on the cards, or reproduce copies by means of a photocopying machine or other copying machine if you have access to one.

Use sturdy paper and trim the cards so that they can be filed along with the commercially produced cards. (See Figure 2-1.)

```
┌─────────────────────────────────────────────┐
│           BUSINESS CARD                       │
│  Name: Finley Conner                          │
│  Firm: Security Investment                    │
│  Purpose of visit: Plan                       │
│  investment program                           │
│  Date: 3/10/--                                │
│      Tel. No. (602) 753-8116                  │
└─────────────────────────────────────────────┘
```

Figure 2-1. Business Calling Card.

For use when caller does not carry a commercially printed card supplied by his employer.

The business card form differs in use from the telephone/visitor message form. (The Telephone/Visitor Message form is discussed and illustrated in Chapter 3, "Office Telephone Calls.") The *business card form* would be used when *no immediate response* to the visit is required. The visit may be an introductory visit—the office visitor may want your boss to know that the firm he represents is a newly organized one or that a new department has been added to the established firm.

The *telephone/visitor message form* would be used when the caller or visitor has *requested a reply*. The reply may be by telephone or letter to acknowledge the call or visit.

Before you usher the visitor to your boss' office, take the

business calling card (or your handwritten note or business card form) to your boss, pronounce the visitor's name, and tell him the purpose of the visit.

The format of the business calling cards varies. A sample calling card is illustrated in Figure 2-2.

Courtesy of International Business Machines Corporation, New York

Figure 2-2. Business Calling Card (Commercial).

You Take the Visitor to Your Boss.   When your boss lets you know that he is free to see the visitor, usher the visitor to your boss' office and announce him: "Mr. Adamson, Mr. Flint of First Shares is here to see you."

If the two have not previously been introduced, you may phrase your introduction in this simple form: "Mr. Adamson, this is Mr. Flint of the First Shares Company."

Introduce Visitors to Your Boss.   Introduce most of the visitors to your boss. This procedure may be too simple, but it seems to be very appropriate for the following reasons.

1. You know your boss' position. You will have pre-determined his importance by your respect for him. You work for him to please him with your office skills and as a representative of the company. Therefore, knowing how important his work is to the company and how valuable his time is, no visitor is as important an individual from the introduction standpoint as is your boss. Your boss' name is mentioned first.

2. If your boss were scheduled to meet the President of the United States, your boss would probably be the one to travel to a specified location. You may never be confronted with the formal presentation, but you should know the proper introduction.

Introduce men to each other by presenting the younger person to the older or more distinguished person; i. e., mention the older or more distinguished person's name first. Follow the same procedure when introducing two women to each other.

A man is introduced to a woman, unless he is a member of the clergy.

The foregoing introduction rules are only to assist you until you have access to a book on etiquette. A recommended source for learning the proper procedures for introducing individuals is the *Business Etiquette Handbook* by the Parker Publishing Company Editorial Staff.

Visitors During Your Boss' Absence.   If a visitor stops in the office "just to say hello" or if he wants to present a proposal for company consideration, make a notation for your boss' information when he returns to the office. If the visitor wishes to leave advertising material with you, make sure that your boss sees it when he returns to the office.

The form used for recording telephone messages may also be used for recording messages from visitors. (See page 38.) Find out where the visitor can be reached at a later time. Your boss may plan to return to the office later the same day and may want to contact the visitor. Ask the visitor to leave his mailing address with you, also. If your boss does not return to the office later in the day, he may want to acknowledge the visit by writing a brief note. (A public relations gesture.)

Attach the visitor's business calling card (if he presents one) to the message form. After your boss reads the message, the calling card may be detached from the message form and filed in the business calling card file.

Hint

You may be able to detect from your boss' reaction to the visitor's name just how important this visit is.

- It may be worthwhile to offer to call your boss'
  wife to tell the cook to set another place for
  dinner.
- If the visit is of a combination business-social air,
  your boss may want to provide transportation
  for the visitor.
- If your boss and the visitor have lunch together
  "out," make a note to ask your boss if the lunch
  is to be included on his expense report.

Of course, none of these items will be mentioned in the
presence or hearing range of the visitor.

The Secretary as Official Hostess to a Woman Visitor. Sometime you will be appointed to meet a visitor of the distaff side of the working world. The purpose of her visit may be an interview with your boss. If she is to remain in the city overnight, in all probability, you will have made hotel or motel reservations for her.

Perhaps the only information you have concerning her visit, other than knowing her name, is the purpose of her visit and where she will be spending the night.

If you have known for several days that you will be transporting her from the terminal, write and tell her how she may identify you. You might suggest a particular place in the terminal where you could meet. Mention the color of your coat or give her some other identifying clue. She most likely will respond in a similar manner.

If you are a "last minute appointee" to meet the visitor, take a good look at her photograph, if one is available. If a photograph is not available, your only clue may be the lost look of a stranger.

The visitor may already be at the terminal when you are notified that you are to meet her and transport her to your office and to her hotel. If this is the situation, call the terminal and speak with the visitor by telephone. Identify yourself and explain that you will be arriving at an approximate time, and describe yourself to her. Ask her how you will identify her. If she has luggage she may appreciate it if you suggest that she check in at the hotel or motel first, instead of going directly to the office from the terminal.

Her schedule as well as yours will determine how much time you spend out of your office, but it could be relaxing for your visitor if time allows you to suggest a cup of tea.

Keeping Appointments. Some of the people wishing to meet with your boss will come to your office in person to make an appointment. The fact that the office visitor has taken time to personally arrange for a meeting with your boss will not necessarily mean that he wants to meet with your boss that same day, unless the visitor does indicate that. However, his appearance may indicate that he would like the meeting to be arranged as soon as possible and for a definite time. The visitor may then tell you which days and the time during the day that he prefers to meet with your boss.

If you cannot discuss this appointment with your boss while the visitor is in your office, ask him to leave a telephone number, or mailing address, if necessary, where he can be reached. This way, you may contact the visitor as soon as the appointment is definitely scheduled. Do not neglect to make a notation on both your calendar and your boss'.

Not all persons who want to visit with your boss at a specified time will make personal appearances. You will no doubt receive appointment requests by telephone and through the mail.

Check your appointment calendar and determine from it what day your boss may possibly be available for the requested appointment. Discuss the appointment request with your boss at the appropriate time. When a definite time has been set aside, confirm the appointment either by telephone (make a notation of the time and day of the conversation) or by letter, whichever method meets with your boss' approval.

Other individuals who request an appointment with your boss may be those who will leave you with no particular day or hour for scheduling an appointment. Included in the conversation may be a statement by the visitor such as, "I'd like to see him within the next two weeks."

Follow through on this request by consulting with your boss as to his preferred day and hour for the appointment, and then confirm the time with the person originating the appointment. Mark your calendar with this scheduled appointment.

Scheduling the appointments may be relatively easy but trying to maintain the day's schedule may test your planning ability at times, particularly if your boss enjoys mingling with the customers, his cohorts or colleagues, and is interested in everything around him. It is not to be assumed that he is avoiding his scheduled appointments; therefore, eliminate your anxiety by locating your boss and reminding him that he has a visitor.

Mark the Calendars.   Mark all appointments on your boss' calendar and also on your own. At the beginning of each day, confirm with your boss the appointments scheduled for the day. Re-confirm with him, periodically, the appointments that have been scheduled for several days or weeks from now. Block off the specified amount of time for the out-of-town visitors as soon as you know the arrival and departure time, if these hours will affect your appointment scheduling practices.

Prime Your Boss.   If your boss has an early appointment, remind him of this before he leaves the office the previous day.

If you have marked your boss' calendar, reminded him verbally of his appointments, and if you have not succeeded in keeping him "on schedule," here's a scheme that has been effective, though not completely foolproof. Call his attention to previously scheduled appointments with *color.*

Color It Blue, Color It Green, Yellow, and Sometimes Red.   If you have access to several colors of plain paper (mimeograph paper works very well), cut the paper to a size that allows ample room for listing the appointments. Type your boss' daily schedule on these different colors of paper. (A former boss welcomed this "colorful trick.")

Head the paper with his name and indicate that this list is a schedule of his appointments for the day. Type the time of day that each appointment is scheduled to arrive; opposite the time, type the name of the visitor and a brief description of the reason for the visit.

Use a different color for each day of the week. For instance, if you use blue on Monday, use yellow for Tuesday, and continue to rotate the colors.

On special days such as Valentine's Day or during the holidays, you might try red paper with white type. (The correction ribbon on your typewriter, if you have such a ribbon, would work fine for this.)

The lists of appointments for the different days of the week will resemble the illustration in Figure 2-3.

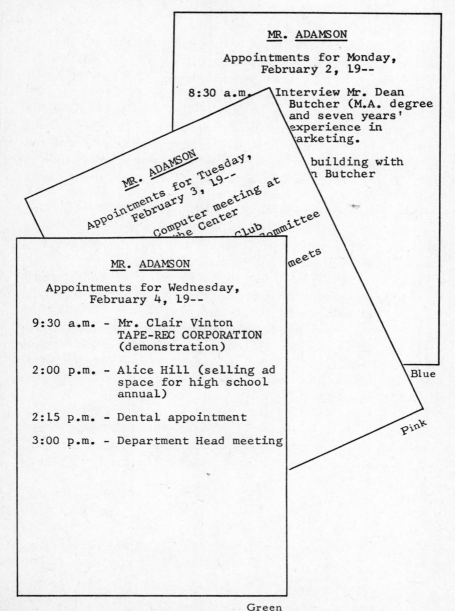

Figure 2-3. Daily Appointment Sheets.

Canceling Visitors' Appointments.   Circumstances may necessitate canceling an appointment for which all arrangements had been made and confirmed.

You may have time to write a letter explaining the reason for the cancellation. Otherwise, telephone the individual and explain the situation.

When distance is a factor, your boss will probably ask you to list several dates so that the appointment may be rescheduled. The visitor may then select the date most convenient for him, since the cancellation was caused through your office.

Pencil a notation on all the suggested dates on your calendar, as a reminder that no out-of-town engagements may be accepted until the pending appointment has been rescheduled and confirmed. When the definite date has been decided upon, indicate this on your calendar. Erase the pencil notations on the other dates which had been tentatively involved.

Cancel Reservations Previously Made for Visitor.   For whatever reason a previously scheduled appointment must be cancelled, the travel arrangements and hotel or motel reservations you have made for the visitor must also be cancelled.

If you made all the arrangements for his travel and overnight accommodations, you must contact the reservations offices so that this space may be made available for others.

Cancel guaranteed hotel or motel reservations immediately.

If you telephone your cancellations, make a notation for your records of the date, time, and the name of the individual handling your cancellation.

Office Telephone Calls

The first self-assignment in this section consists of two parts. (1) Look for the telephone directory supplied by the system that serves your city. Keep it in a convenient place for *your* use only. (2) Obtain a list of the names and numbers of other company departments. You may need to contact someone in another department, at your boss' request, without delay.

Answering the Telephone.   In a small office, you may be answering the telephone every time it rings. The telephone call may be for your boss or for anyone in your office.

If you work for a large company, you will probably answer the telephone only when calls are relayed to your office through a switchboard.

Find out exactly how you are to answer the telephone. Are you expected to answer the telephone with the "Good morning" and "Good afternoon" greetings before saying the company name?

A business firm may include the name of the city in its official name, but because of the length of its official name, may request that the name of the city be omitted when answering the telephone.

The company for which you work may insist that the official name be used when you answer the telephone. If the word "The" is a part of the official name, you would then speak every word that forms the name of the company, for example, "The Circle Globe Company."

If the company for which you work permits those answering the telephone to drop the word "The," you should use the same phrase that others are instructed to speak when acknowledging the ring of the telephone.

The Secretary's Identity.   When you answer the telephone for your boss' office, find out whether or not you are to identify yourself. If your boss does want you to identify yourself, a suggested greeting is: "Mr. Adamson's office, Miss Raffold speaking." If you are not required to identify yourself, the suggested greeting may be to simply identify your boss' office— "Mr. Adamson's office."

Answer the telephone in the manner that suits your boss.

Screening Telephone Calls.   If you are not expected to screen your boss' calls, in all probability, the calls will be routed directly to your boss' office and he will answer his own telephone.

If you are expected to screen the telephone calls, the system may be set up so that all of your boss' calls are put through on your office telephone enabling you to announce the calls through a special signaling device.

Not all of the callers will identify themselves so you must then secure the caller's name, the firm he represents, the location of the firm, and the reason for the call. Instead of a direct, "Who's calling?" or an abrupt, "What's your name?" a less pungent approach may be, "May I tell Mr. Adamson who is calling, please?"

Your boss may not always be available to speak with the party calling. If he is out of the office, simply tell the party calling that your boss is out of the office. Offer to have your boss return the call, or ask if you may take a message. (Unless you have been specifically instructed to volunteer explanations of your boss' absence, the only information available to the party calling should be the date you expect him to return to the office.)

Before the Telephone Call Is Transferred.   You may want to automatically transfer a telephone call from your office to another department if you know that the subject matter is ordinarily handled there. When a call is specifically directed to your boss, let him know this before you automatically transfer the call. Your boss may have some important information relating to the particular telephone call. Although he may instruct you to transfer the call to another individual, he *should* be made aware of the call.

The Telephone Call for an Appointment. If the person calling wants to arrange an appointment with your boss, but is hesitant in revealing the purpose of his visit, you may suggest that he give you some idea of his reason so that you will be able to set aside ample time for him. Unless your boss is willing to see everyone who requests his time, tell the party calling that you will confirm his appointment. If the telephone call is a long distance call, try to confirm the appointment immediately. Telephone calls from within the city should be confirmed the same day. Discuss the requested appointments with your boss, then notify the individuals who requested appointments as to whether the appointment is a confirmed one or if another time has been suggested.

The Traveling Telephone Call. Business activity reports may be directed first to your office, where you, in turn, are to relay these reports to other departments.

Make a notation on your recorded telephone message of the time of day and to whom you conveyed the information.

Recording Incoming Telephone Calls. If your office does not have a printed form for recording incoming telephone calls, a form similar to Figure 3-1 may serve your office needs. The design is simple and can be used to record messages from office visitors as well as to provide a record of telephone calls.

Presenting the Telephone Messages to Your Boss. Present the telephone messages to your boss according to his wishes. He may want the calls arranged according to the hour of the day they were received by you. If he requests them in that order, he undoubtedly returns the telephone calls in the order in which they were received timewise. Or he may prefer to have messages assembled according to *importance* or *urgency,* as derived by you. If this is the arrangement he prefers, he may return a call which you recorded only a few minutes ago rather than the first call you recorded (which may have been recorded more than two hours ago). To be sure of his preference, ask him.

Compiling the Boss' Special Directory. After the telephone calls have been presented to your boss and either he or you have followed up on the messages or requests, save the recording slips. From the information recorded on these slips, you will be able to

```
┌─────────────────────────────────────────────┐
│              M E S S A G E                    │
│          ─────────────────────────────        │
│   TO: _____        │
│        Date: _____ Time:_____         │
│   FROM: _____(Name of person)_____ *          │
│         _____(Firm Represented)_____         │
│         _____(City)_____, _(State)_           │
│   Telephone                                    │
│     Number: _____/_____          │
│              Area Code                         │
│   * TELEPHONED/VISITED THE OFFICE              │
│   (Message) _____        │
│                                                │
│         _____       │
│                                                │
│         PLEASE CALL HIM   ┌──┐                 │
│                           └──┘                 │
│         By: _____        │
└─────────────────────────────────────────────┘
```

Figure 3-1. Telephone/Visitor Message Form.

compile a business telephone directory for your boss. List in the directory the name, firm, address, and telephone number. This directory may be arranged alphabetically, geographically, or according to the type of business.

You may want to include a separate section for recording addresses and telephone numbers of his personal friends. This will be a convenient list to use when mailing holiday greetings and for arranging special get-togethers.

Placing Business Telephone Calls.   Anytime that you, as the secretary, dial or push the buttons on the telephone to carry out your boss' order of relaying information to another person, follow a procedure similar to the one below, regardless of where the party with whom you wish to speak maintains his office—in a skyscraper or in his home.

Identify your office and your position within the office:

> Hello, I'm Mrs. Marshall, secretary to Mr. Bilton of Bilton and Zante Corporation. May I speak with Mr. Penn?

A homemaker who answers the telephone for her husband could easily become annoyed at the unbusiness-like manner: "Is Frank there?" even though she may recognize the voice as being that of the office secretary. Such an approach by a secretary may trigger a question-answer period; and the respect for the business office from which the call originated could be "diluted" by the time the message is relayed to the proper person.

The immediate identification of the caller seems to radiate a tone of efficiency. The response to the call will be a pleasant and prompt one. Efficiency establishes good business relationships both between offices, and between home and office.

Offer to Assist the Callers.   After you have been a part of the business firm for an appreciable amount of time, you will know what information is confidential and what is not. Offer to assist the caller. Find out specifically what he wants to know. If you have access to the information, although it may take ten minutes or more to compile the facts for him, offer to return his call. Most callers are pleased to have a call returned if they are simply told that you will try to answer their questions and admit that it will take some time.

Long Distance Telephone Calls.   It may be necessary to place a long distance telephone call for your boss, so find out to which telephones you will have access for this purpose and learn the numbers of those telephones.

If the line is not clear and you have difficulty hearing the person with whom you are trying to converse, let the operator know this before continuing the call. To ask a caller to repeat his name several times or to ask him to spell his name more than one time can be disconcerting to him. If you can't hear clearly, your boss will have the same difficulty, and this could result in less than the most favorable company relations. Even though the party calling may hear you very distinctly, he will be much more patient when he knows the connection is not clear at your end of the line.

Telephone Service.   If you do not know the telephone

number of the firm or an individual in a distant city, service is provided to help you.

American Telephone and Telegraph Company described the procedure for securing a distant telephone number as follows:

> Directory Assistance (Information) can be obtained without charge by dialing the appropriate Area Code plus 555-1212.

In addition, American Telephone and Telegraph Company provided this information:

> ... specific dialing directions for Directory Assistance as well as other types of calls are contained in the "Call Guide" (or "Introductory") pages of the telephone directory.

Follow the directions outlined in the telephone directory for reporting incorrectly dialed numbers.

Time-saving information is listed in the telephone directory. Read it.

Long Distance Call Record.   Some companies request that all Long Distance telephone calls be recorded. Persons authorized to place Long Distance telephone calls may be supplied with a pad-type form, or an entirely different procedure may be followed.

A pad-type Long Distance Call Record form may resemble Figure 3-2.

```
┌─────────────────────────────────────────────────────┐
│              LONG DISTANCE CALL RECORD                │
│   TO: _____ (Person and   │
│       _____   Firm)       │
│                                                       │
│       _____,  _____             │
│            City              State                    │
│       Telephone Number                                │
│            Called (include Area Code) ___/_____   │
│   REASON FOR CALLING: _____   │
│       _____  │
│       _____  │
│                                                       │
│   CALL PLACED BY: _____   │
│                       Department: _____       │
│   TIME: _____                                    │
│   CHARGES: _____                                   │
└─────────────────────────────────────────────────────┘
```

Figure 3-2. Long Distance Call Record.

4

Correspondence Demands Action

Mail will be delivered to your office every day, and you may be responsible for handling every piece of it that comes to your desk. This could include reading it, routing it, acknowledging it, searching for data to answer it, but never discarding any of it—at least not until your boss has had a chance to see it.

Find out what time the mail is delivered to your office, as well as how many times a day it is delivered.

Clear Your Desk. Before opening the mail, clear your desk of any papers and folders, to prevent it from lodging in a wrong folder or being swept up with unrelated material.

PREVENT PAPER PYRAMIDS

For every First Class letter that comes in, most secretaries want a First Class letter to go out that same day. The mail is current when this happens.

To help your boss keep his desk uncluttered, you must develop a system which will keep the mail moving.

Your boss may give you specific instructions concerning the mail. If he hasn't given you any instructions in processing the mail, the following suggestions may help you.

Check the Mail Labels. As you sort the mail, check the addressee label to make sure that no mail in your office is addressed to another individual or department. If the address label shows an incorrect mailing address for the company, or if your boss wants certain material to be sent to his home, prepare a Change of Address form and forward it to the sender.

If the company has recently moved to a new location, it might be a time-saver to prepare several copies of the Change of Address form (Figure 4-1).

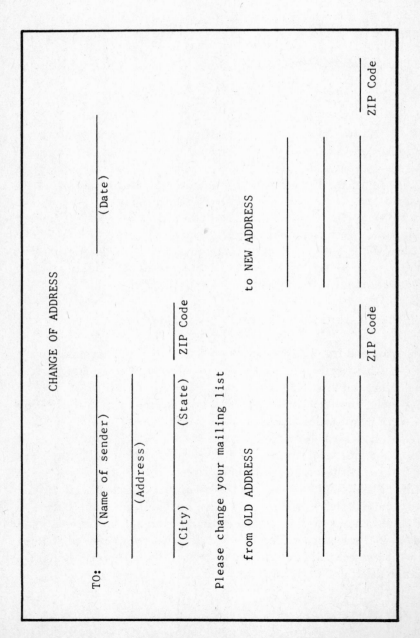

Figure 4-1. Change of Address Form.

Sort the Mail. Generally the mail can be sorted into First Class mail, personal, bills due, newspapers, and magazines.

Do not discard the envelopes; attach them to the correspondence. A return address may not appear on a letter or other correspondence. Or, material sent to your boss may not have a cover letter. The return address on the envelope may enable your boss and you to identify the sender.

Stamp the Mail. Stamp the date it was received on every piece of mail. Be consistent when date-stamping the mail, i.e., if you stamp one letter in the upper right-hand corner near the edge of the letter, stamp all incoming mail on the upper right corner. Maybe you will prefer affixing the date stamp on the back of letters.

Gather the Information Needed to Answer the Mail. *To do something* even though there may be "loose ends to tie" when your boss has had time to study the mail will be *better than to do nothing.*

Almost every First Class letter will require some preliminary preparation before it can be answered. The responsibility for gathering the necessary information rests with you. If previous correspondence relating to the subject has been filed, pull the pertinent material from the file and attach it to the letter, for your boss' briefing.

The importance of the letter will determine its position for receiving attention. Put the most important correspondence on top before you take it to your boss.

What the Mail Might Include. The mail might include letters requesting your boss to be guest speaker at special functions; letters of inquiry regarding employment possibilities; letters seeking information regarding an individual's credit rating or character analysis on a personal basis. The mail may include official notices of meetings and conventions. Former employees may ask for a letter of recommendation to assist them in securing a new position. Requests for monetary donations may be directed to your office for any number of reasons; e.g., community projects headed by your boss, or charity for a local situation.

Read every word of every letter. With a blue pencil underline the "message" presented in each letter. Begin NOW to take care of as many details as you possible can.

Speaking Engagements.   Details concerning speaking engagements and out-of-town meetings are outlined in Chapter 16, which is devoted to the business trip. That section features the form designed for speaking engagements and meetings. Refer also to Chapter 13, "Structural Reminder System," for follow-up details.

Following the confirmation of a speaking engagement, mail to the individual who is corresponding in behalf of the organization, group, or club a personal data summary and a photograph which can be reproduced. (This is good for public relations and serves as introductory material to the community or city visited.)

Photographs should be mailed between cardboard or other heavy paper. Photographs should be returned to the sender after they have served their purpose. (We must economize.)

If your boss makes personal appearances as a speaker, it would be wise to prepare his personal data summary on a stencil, or other paper used for reproducing several copies.

When travel arrangements are made, write a letter to the organization head or to whomever contacted your office originally and advise him of the travel plans, as well as the time of your boss' arrival and departure.

Letters of Application.   The applicant whose letter impresses your boss may be asked to visit the company for a personal interview. When the date and time have been agreed upon, reserve this time for the interview. Make a notation on the calendar that you use for daily appointments, and also mark both your boss' calendar and the calendar which has all the days of the month on one page. Label a folder with the pertinent information concerning the interview—name, date, time, position—and put the correspondence in the folder. Then file the folder in the Follow-Up section of the filing cabinet.

Credit Ratings or Character Analysis.   Before answering a letter of inquiry about the business habits of a customer, your boss will probably want to know the length of time the individual has been a customer, the amounts of money owed, and the promptness with which he meets his obligations.

Comments concerning the individual's character may reflect his sense of responsibility to his personal commitments and his community, his integrity, and his conduct in general.

The information your office supplies will depend on the

questions asked or statements made in the letter addressed to your boss.

Recommendation for Former Employee. A prospective employer may question an applicant's former employer about the applicant's qualifications as they relate to a certain position.

To help organize your boss' reply, he may want to know how long the individual was employed by the company, his productiveness as related to the duties assigned to him, and his attitude toward fellow employees; his adaptability and his capacity to learn.

Here, again, the questions asked will determine the information you should look for. Gather as much available information from the records as you can.

Notice of Meeting. If the communication is an official notice of a meeting and you have learned from your boss that he will attend, make a notation on the calendars, as referred to in Chapter 13, "Structural Reminder System." Indicate on the communication that you have marked the calendars. Block off sufficient time prior to the scheduled meeting hour to allow your boss time to drive, park, and reach the meeting room on time.

If your boss is unable to attend the meeting, indicate this on the communication along with his reason (if he volunteers one) for not attending. Your boss may instruct you to telephone the chairman of the group which is to meet and explain his absence.

Donations. Many busy executives contribute time and effort to help build better communities; they assume various responsibilities for civic organizations; they assist organizations in worthwhile projects. Sometimes monetary contributions are accepted for the program in lieu of personal service.

Make a record for these donations similar to Figure 4-2.

Nonprofit organizations sometimes receive gifts. If your boss serves on a committee for a nonprofit organization and the gifts are delivered to your office, keep a record of these gifts. If the gift is designated by the contributor to be used for a specific project or purpose, indicate on the record the amount that is stipulated for a specific fund.

The record is similar to the record used for the list of donations. There are slight changes in the headings (Figure 4-3).

Personal Mail. Mail addressed to your boss with the word

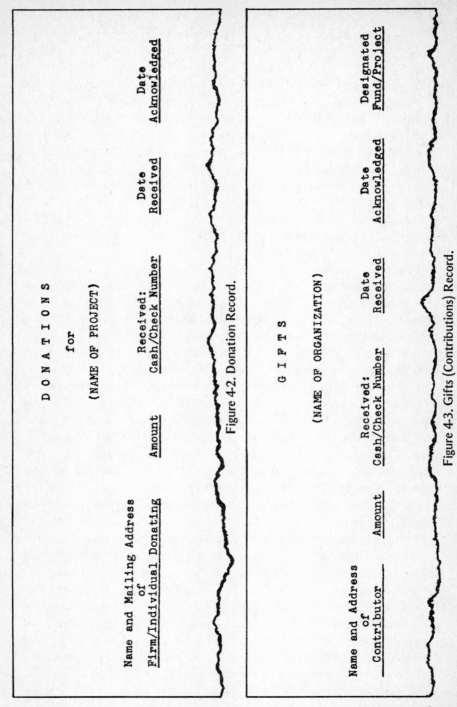

Figure 4-2. Donation Record.

Figure 4-3. Gifts (Contributions) Record.

46

"Personal" typed or written on the envelope should be placed in a folder that is labeled "Personal Mail." Whenever you take the mail in to your boss, call his attention to the personal mail so that it won't be shoved aside or mixed in with other papers on his desk.

Bills or Payments Due. Any statements of amounts due should be sorted into two stacks. One stack would be those bills that are paid from his personal account. The other stack would be those bills that are paid by the company or paid from another account. The bills paid from his personal account may then be placed in the folder with his other personal mail.

Printed Material. Newspapers, newsletters, and reports should be scanned for pertinent facts and other articles that may interest your boss. Outline the article if it is not a lengthy one. If the article is several pages in length, attach lightweight signals to the pages on which the article continues. Open the newspaper, or magazine, to the page of interest. Other articles in the same periodical may also be marked for his attention by the signals mentioned above.

With a blue pencil, underline the main points in short articles and brief reports.

Condense the more detailed reports by summarizing the important statements and facts. Type the summary on a separate sheet of paper. Topics which interest him may be quickly spotted on your summary sheet when it is presented to your boss. On the summary sheet, opposite the topic, list the page number of the report on which the topic appears.

Circulated Mail. Your boss may subscribe to periodicals which he feels may be of interest to others in the company. The same people may be on the "circulation list" each time the printed material is received in your office. Perhaps the material is filed in the office of the person named last on the list. Or your boss may ask that it be returned to his office, where you are responsible for filing the material.

If the same people are to receive the periodical each time the issue is received in your office, prepare a "Circulation Slip" and attach this to the periodical. After your boss has read the periodical, it will be ready for circulation. If the periodical is to be returned to you for filing, indicate that it is to be returned, on the "Circulation Slip."

A carbon copy of the "Circulation Slip," which may be filed in your reminder file (or spindled), would be an aid in tracing the periodical should your boss ask for it before it completes the route specified.

Figure 4-4 is the form which has been termed the "Circulation Slip."

```
            CIRCULATION SLIP
                  Date: _____

From:      Paul J. Adamson

Subject:  Weekly Report


Please read, initial, and pass this
around.
            Nyberg      _____
            Williams    _____
            Marshall    _____
            Martley     _____
            Peebler     _____
    FILE: Return to Paul J. Adamson


    PJA:ar
```

Figure 4-4. Circulation Slip.

The Mail: From Your Desk to Your Boss' Desk.   Your boss' schedule will determine whether or not you need a "system" for calling the mail to his attention: (a) If your boss has designated a certain time for answering the mail each day, you may be able to process the mail and present it to him in order of the communication's importance, without placing it in separate folders; (b) If there is no specified time for answering the mail each day, place the sorted mail in labeled folders.

The Mail Summary Sheet.   The system for handling the mail when your boss leaves the city may differ from the system used when he is in the city. The length of time he plans to be out of the office and out of the city may also determine which procedure will be the most effective for taking care of the mail.

The same kind of mail—First Class, personal, bills, and magazines—will reach your office no matter where your boss is, in or out of town.

Taking care of the mail during the time your boss is out of the city will be similar, in detail, to what you do when your boss is in the office. The details described in the preceding pages are: (1) Sort the mail; (2) Check the address labels for completeness and correctness; (3) Re-route mail not intended for your department; (4) Open and stamp the mail.

A different procedure to consider is summarizing the mail. The Mail Summary sheet might save your boss "reading" time when he does return to the office. It could also be an opportunity for you to become familiar with the pending business transactions. To summarize the mail, extract the main points and put these "in writing"—you will remember having received certain letters when reference is made to them weeks later.

Many executives telephone their secretaries while they are in another city; and they expect their secretary to brief them on the mail received and the messages left for them.

When your boss telephones your office, he may dictate an answer to a letter, or he may say, "Hold it until I get back—don't do anything until then."

The Mail Summary sheet could also serve as a record of the mail received. Write what you have done "on your own" in the column headed "What Has Been Done." Write down any instructions your boss gives you concerning a particular communication discussed during the telephone conversation.

The Mail Summary sheet is shown in Figure 4-5.

Forwarding Letters.   Establish this policy and enforce it: *The original letter remains in the office.* Exception: Your boss' request.

If your boss *must* have the original and he asks you to forward it to him, copy the letter. Indicate on the copy that the original was mailed to him. (He undoubtedly will tell you why he needs

MAIL SUMMARY

Date Received	Received From:	Subject Matter	What Has Been Done

NOTE: When listing the mail received, begin with the First-Class mail.

Figure 4-5. Mail Summary Sheet.

the original letter; and you could pencil the reason on the copy.)

If your boss doesn't need the original letter but is anxious to read the letter, copy it and send him the copy. Make a notation on the original letter that a copy was sent to him. Show the date the copy was mailed and to where it was mailed.

This practice will help eliminate a search for "lost" letters.

Acknowledge the Letters. Acknowledge *most* of the First Class mail. Perhaps no specific instructions have been left with you prior to your boss' departure, but you know that he will be away for several days and you also know that you will not be talking with him during his absence from the office.

A simple acknowledgment to the person sending the letter to your boss will tell him that it reached its destination and that some time will elapse before he receives an answer in detail.

Letters acknowledging mail while your boss is out of the office follow:

1.

(Date)

(Address)

Dear _____ :
Your letter of March 12 arrived after Mr. Adamson left on a business trip. I will call his attention to it when he returns on the twenty-seventh of March.

Sincerely yours,

2.

(Date)

(Address)

Dear _____ :
Mr. Adamson is out of the office until the second week in March. When he returns I will see to it that your letter is brought to his attention.

Sincerely yours,

When a "Personal" letter addressed to your boss is delivered to the office, it should not be opened by you. Stamp the date it was received on the envelope.

If the return address on the envelope is complete, you might write the sender the following letter.

(Date)

(Address)

Dear Mr. Jones:
Your letter postmarked January 12, 19-- which is marked for the personal attention of Mr. Adamson arrived in our office this morning.
Mr. Adamson is not expected in the office until the sixteenth of April; at that time, I will call his attention to it.

Sincerely yours,

Instead of acknowledging a *letter demanding action,* hold it until you have specific instructions from your boss on what to do. Unless you know all the details, and even if you think you know all of the details, the letter should be called to your boss' attention first. To acknowledge the letter might create an uncomfortable situation for your boss.

The Secretary's Signature.   Shown below are samples of autographs and typed signatures as they appear on business letters signed by secretaries.

Single Woman

Autograph: *Ann McCord* or *(Miss) Ann McCord*

Typed Signature: Ann McCord

Married *or* **Widowed Woman**

Autograph: *Ann McCord Allison*

Typed Signature: Mrs. Ann McCord Allison

or

Autograph: *Ann M. Allison*

Typed Signature: (Mrs. Gregory B. Allison)

or

Autograph: *(Mrs.) Ann McCord Allison*

Typed Signature: Ann McCord Allison

Divorced Woman who retains the surname of her former husband

Autograph: *(Mrs.) Suzanne D. Hatch*

Typed Signature: Suzanne D. Hatch

Divorced Woman who reverts to the use of her maiden name

Autograph: *(Miss) Suzanne Dalton*

Typed Signature: Suzanne Dalton

Many times the title is typed along with the signature, such as *Miss Suzanne Dalton*, thereby eliminating the parentheses. The autograph is merely Suzanne Dalton.

Mail Route Slip. Your boss should be the first person to see all correspondence addressed to him after you have opened the mail.

Every piece of mail addressed specifically to your boss deserves his attention, even if his "attention" is only a nod of his head (to indicate that he has seen it) along with an instruction to route it to another individual or department for disposition.

Before any mail leaves your office, transfer the pertinent information to a Mail Route Slip. This slip could be typed in duplicate; it would then serve as a record and filed in the appropriate location.

The Mail Route Slip is very brief, and it would be used when the material routed to another department or individual is not to be returned to your office.

A simple form that can be duplicated might be set up similar to the one shown in Figure 4-6.

Meetings and Conventions. Meeting notices and convention notices are mailed several weeks or months prior to the scheduled

MAIL ROUTE SLIP

(Name of Department)

TO: Purchasing Department

Attention: O. Brime

Date: November 6

S U B J E C T:

MAGAZINE FOR CONTRACTORS

Remarks: Let me know if you
are interested in the ad on
page 56.

P. Adamson, V.P.

Figure 4-6. Mail Route Slip.

date. How much your boss enjoys traveling and attending various gatherings will determine how you handle this type of correspondence. Call his attention to these notices immediately if he enjoys meetings and if he plans to attend as many as can be worked into his schedule.

Ask about travel arrangements and reservations as soon as you learn of his wish to attend the scheduled meeting or convention. Begin to make plans for his out-of-town trips without delay, because the time a "traveling" executive spends in the office will leave little time to discuss details. Consider, also, that much of his time in the office will be set aside for meetings with business associates and department heads.

Analyze the Mail Situation.   It will be your responsibility to see that the mail does not pile up.

How much time your boss spends in the office, how much time he allows each day for dictating answers to letters, and the amount of time you are allowed just to call his attention to the mail for specific instructions will be factors in selecting the most effective system for handling the mail.

Perhaps the most effective method to employ day by day would be the same procedures that are described for handling the mail when your boss is out of town—the summarizing system.

The suggestions for processing the mail in the preceding pages by no means touch on every type of request or correspondence that any one office will receive; but by training oneself to grasp the pertinent points in the correspondence, the time spent in the boss' office for going through the mail can be very brief.

The more "research" you do in order that the mail can be answered correctly and quickly, the more time your boss will have for the major projects which demand his consideration and executive-level decisions.

In a short period of time you may be drafting letters for your boss' approval, and the real thrill will come when you draft a letter that meets his approval, and the president signs it.

5

Inter office Correspondence

Home offices correspond with branch offices, branch offices correspond with other branch offices, departments exchange correspondence, and so on. This correspondence between divisions under the same management or ownership is termed interoffice correspondence.

Interoffice memorandums may be designed to match the company letterhead, or they may be a variation of the letterhead—perhaps the emblem will not be as decorative, or the size of the paper will be smaller—but still identifiable as a memorandum.

An interoffice memorandum will not bear a complete mailing address; a greeting will not appear on the interoffice memorandum, nor will it bear a complimentary closing. Enclosures and carbon copy notations may be indicated on the interoffice memorandum just as they are typed at the end of a letter.

The interoffice memorandum is not reserved for any specific subject. Use the memorandum to notify employees of newly adopted procedures, personnel transfers, office achievements and awards, and to notify personnel involved in conducting tours of the buildings, if tours are conducted for interested groups.

If your office has no form and you find that you use this system of communication frequently, it might be well to begin using one of the convenient forms designed by commercial printers.

A sample form has been furnished by Woehrmyer Printing Company, Denver, Colorado and is illustrated in Figure 5-1.

Not all persons who have responsible positions have access to secretarial services at all times. Company personnel who spend a

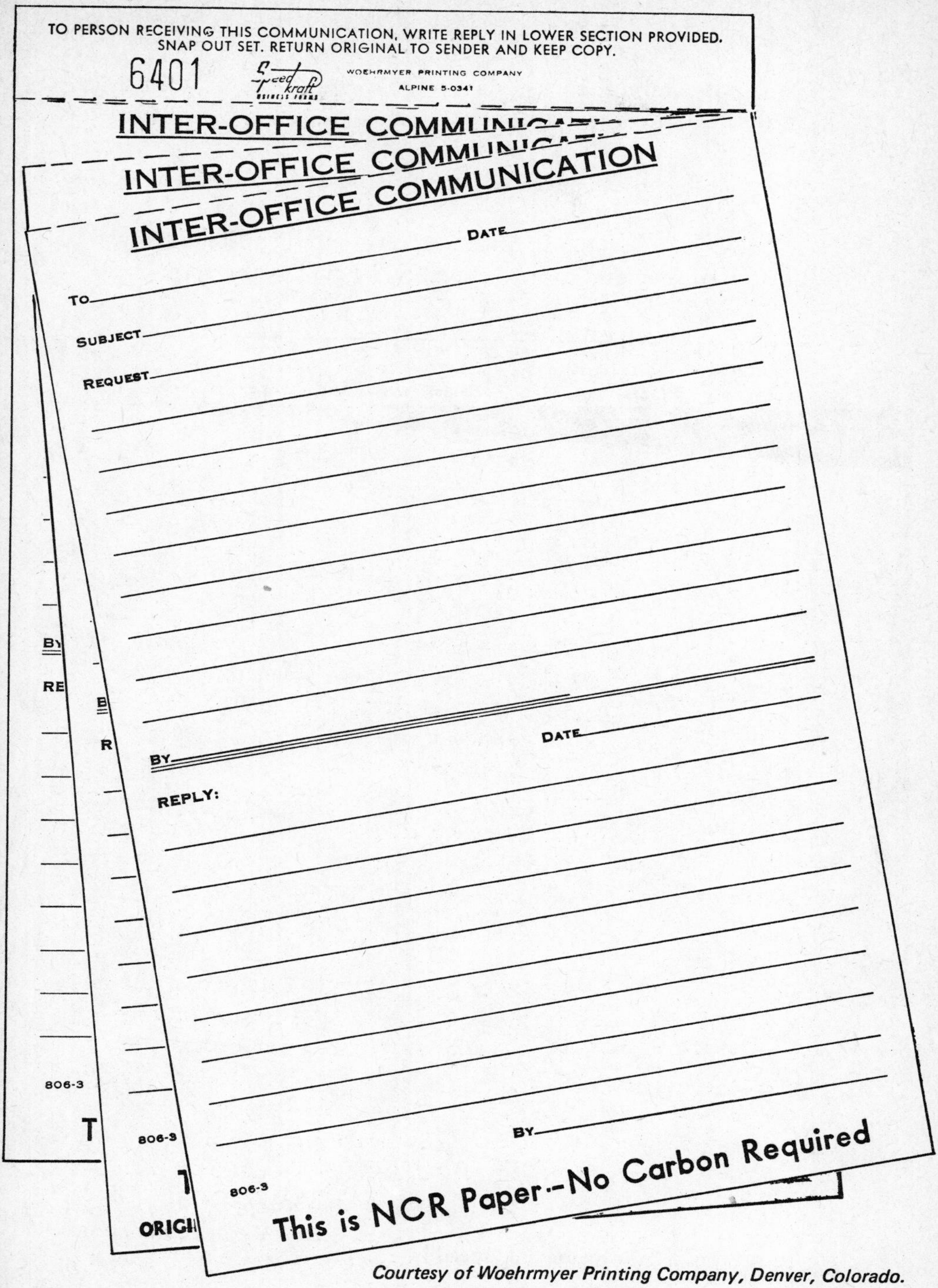

TO PERSON RECEIVING THIS COMMUNICATION, WRITE REPLY IN LOWER SECTION PROVIDED.
SNAP OUT SET. RETURN ORIGINAL TO SENDER AND KEEP COPY.

6401   *Speed kraft*   WOEHRMYER PRINTING COMPANY
ALPINE 5-0341

INTER-OFFICE COMMUNICATION

INTER-OFFICE COMMUNICATION

INTER-OFFICE COMMUNICATION

INTER-OFFICE COMMUNICATION

DATE

TO

SUBJECT

REQUEST

BY

RE

B

R

BY   DATE

REPLY:

BY

806-3

806-3

806-3

T

ORIGI

This is NCR Paper—No Carbon Required

Courtesy of Woehrmyer Printing Company, Denver, Colorado.

Figure 5-1. Inter office Communication.

57

considerable amount of time away from the office may not want to wait until they return to the office to take care of correspondence.

Paper and carbon packets are available for written communications.

Wilson Jones Company of Chicago has supplied the form which is illustrated in Figure 5-2. On the reverse side of the form there is

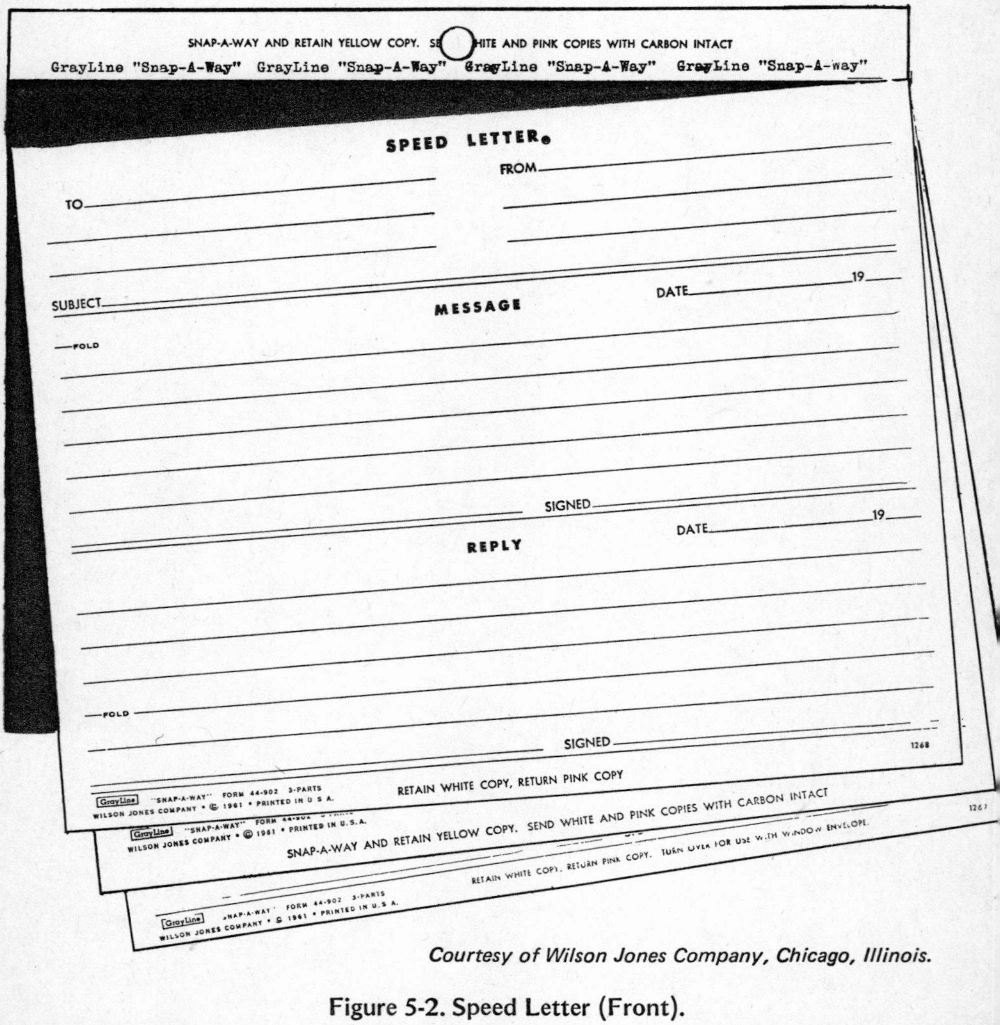

Courtesy of Wilson Jones Company, Chicago, Illinois.

Figure 5-2. Speed Letter (Front).

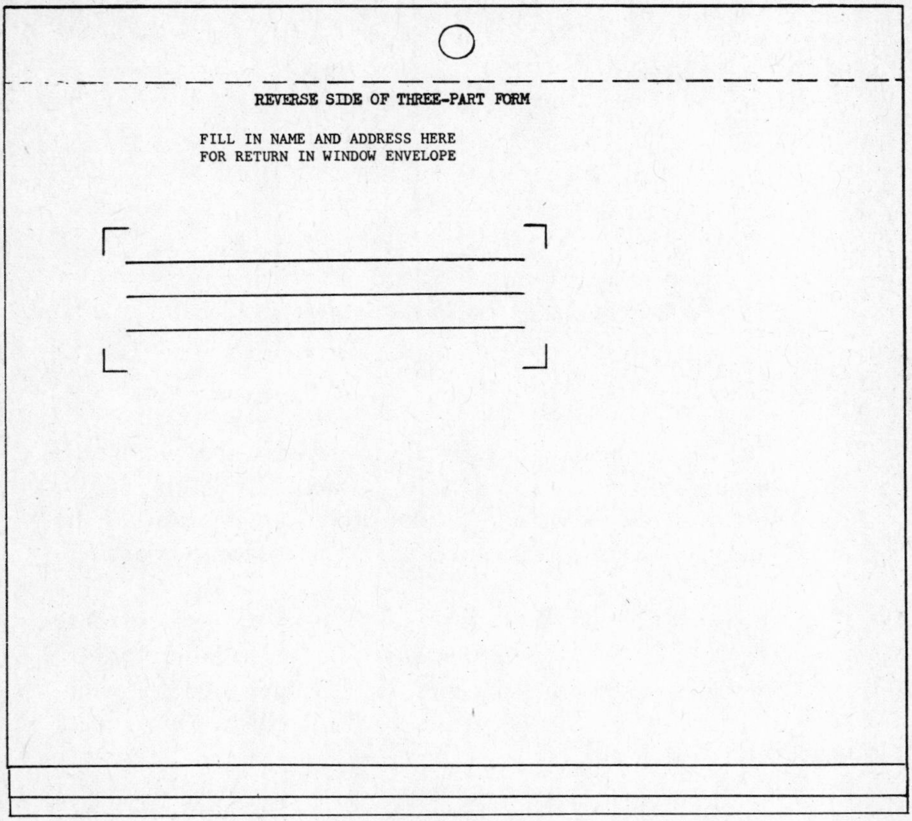

REVERSE SIDE OF THREE-PART FORM

FILL IN NAME AND ADDRESS HERE
FOR RETURN IN WINDOW ENVELOPE

Courtesy of Wilson Jones Company, Chicago, Illinois.

Figure 5-2. Speed Letter (Back).

a blocked area for the address and a fold line so that the sheet will fit properly in a window envelope when a reply is made to the original communication.

Be sure a supply of envelopes and stamps are available so that communication forms will serve the purpose for which they are intended.

6

Dictation Notations

There may be a special time of day every day that your boss prefers for answering mail and dictating other material to you. Of course, you must be prepared to take dictation any time of the day and for any length of time because the dictation sessions will vary.

Your boss may use dictation to answer letters, prepare agreements, record minutes of meetings, make special announcements to personnel, prepare speeches, or relay pertinent information to be transmitted to other offices. All such dictation requires accuracy and neatness.

Your shorthand pad and pens should always be in a convenient place in your desk so that you won't have to search for them when you are called in to take dictation.

DICTATION DETAILS

Always take more than one pen with you when you prepare for the dictation session. Also take a pencil with you; be sure your shorthand pad has more than a few clean pages left in it so that you won't run out of paper in the middle of a sentence.

You may want to write yourself a one-word note on a particular document or letter, or remind yourself to correct a typographical error. Have a pencil handy so that you can make this notation, lightly. The pencil notation will be just a reminder; it is not intended to serve as a permanent change. A pencil notation can be easily erased, but an ink notation can ruin the entire paper, even if the correction is *one* letter in the alphabet.

Some secretaries may prefer to take dictation with a pencil. Others prefer a fine point fluid ink pen. The fluid ink characters are permanent and remain legible.

Record Date of Dictation.   Date every page of your short-hand pad at the bottom of the page. Write down the month, day, and year. There may be a time that a letter had not reached its destination or has been lost in the addressee's office. Perhaps the date was unintentionally omitted (it does happen!) and the date is a necessary part of a pending agreement or contract. By dating every page of your shorthand pad each time you take dictation, you will be able to retrace work that originated in your office.

End-of-letter Symbols.   Devise some symbol to indicate the end of each letter or other material dictated. The symbol must be one that is easily and quickly written. You might find it easier to skip a line between the dictated material.

Figure 6-1 illustrates some simple samples of end-of-letter symbols. You may already be using a symbol which adequately identifies the end of dictated material and which indicates the end of one letter and the beginning of another letter.

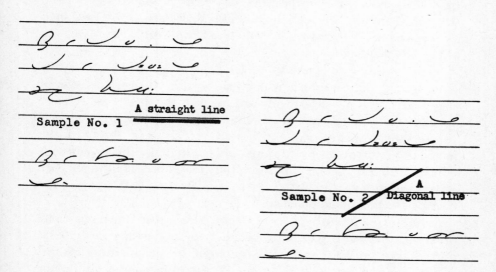

Figure 6-1. End-of-Letter Symbols.

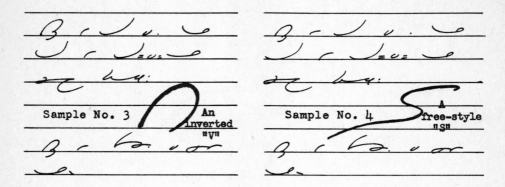

Sample No. 3 — An inverted "V"

Sample No. 4 — A free-style "S"

Figure 6-1. End-of-Letter Symbols (continued).

Signify "Rush" Letters. Prepare yourself for an occasional "rush" letter. The "rush" letter may be dictated at the same sitting that several other letters are dictated. You must signify which letter or letters will be typed immediately after the dictation session.

One way to readily recognize a "rush" letter is to turn the page of your shorthand pad on which the letter appears, and crease this page diagonally so that the bottom of the page extends beyond the right-hand side of your shorthand pad (Figure 6-2). The sketch shows what the page would look like if a "rush" letter were to appear on the creased page.

Another way to indicate that a letter is to be typed immediately is to use the plastic signals which can be slipped over the edge of the page in your shorthand pad on which the "rush" letter appears. (The signals can be purchased at office supply stores.) Of course you probably will not know when a "rush" letter will be included in the dictation sessions. Unless you take the signals with you each time you take dictation, they may not serve the purpose of indicating a "rush" letter as conveniently as just creasing the page of the shorthand pad.

For Want of a Word. . . . If you have missed a word, a part of a dictated sentence, or if you do not understand a dictated phrase, wait until the dictator has completed his dictation, instead of interrupting him. After he has finished dictating the letter or speech, tell him which part of the dictated material is not

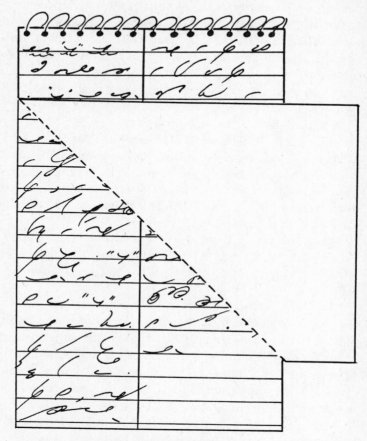

Figure 6-2. Signifies "Rush" Letter.

Page of Shorthand Pad Creased Diagonally to Indicate "Rush" Letter.

complete in your shorthand. Then, by reading your notes to him, he will probably remember exactly what words he spoke earlier.

Do not guess what the word or phrase could be. Some bosses prefer to dictate another sentence than be presented with a typed letter that is incorrect in wording and meaning.

The Complimentary Close. The first letter your boss dictates to you will be the time to find out what complimentary close he uses on his general correspondence. This will also be the time to find out exactly how he signs his letters. Does he sign his full name, or does he prefer to use initials with his surname?

Dictation "Breaks."   Breaks in dictation are opportune times for you to reread your notes, rewrite a not-too-good shorthand character, and to insert punctuation marks. A dictation break, as a result of a telephone call or a brief visit with a vacationing business associate, may also enable you to list one or two new words.

Dictation Builds Your Vocabulary.   Dictation sessions can be vocabulary builders for secretaries. Make a list of the words your boss uses that are unfamiliar to you; look up these new words in the dictionary for pronunciation, correct spelling, and meaning. Also look up these new words in your shorthand dictionary to learn the shorthand character, and practice writing the words in shorthand.

Taking Dictation from More Than One Person.   You may be called upon to take dictation from someone other than your boss.

At the close of the dictation, write the dictator's initials, for reference.

Canceling Transcribed Material.   Cancel the shorthand notes that are transcribed by either drawing a diagonal line through the material or by making an "X" through the shorthand characters.

If you have a number of letters to transcribe, count the number of end-of-letter symbols in your shorthand pad and compare that number with your transcribed letters, for assurance that you have not missed transcribing any of the letters.

Transcribing Dictated Material Several Days Later.   If your boss travels several days of the week, you may spend an entire day taking dictation. You may not be able to transcribe the dictated material until the following day. Or it may take two or three days to complete the transcription. If this arrangement exists in your office, indicate the date that the dictation was transcribed, and also show the date the material was dictated, in your shorthand pad. This will give you a record of the date correspondence was mailed, assuming the correspondence was mailed on the same date that it was transcribed.

Typing Rough-Draft Material.   Material that is to be typed in rough copy should be double-spaced; and ample margins, for insertions or corrections, should be the rule.

7

Good Letter Form and Style

Letterhead designs vary, as do the kinds of businesses. The style, or form, of business letter varies. The style used in your office may be governed by company preference.

Some companies may request that the same letter style be used throughout its offices. Other business firms might allow their secretaries to use whichever letter style each prefers. A business firm with four secretaries may send out four business letters, not one of the letters identical in style, or form. Neatness and accuracy may be the business' major concern.

POSITIONING PARTS OF THE LETTER

If you work in an office that does not distribute handbooks designating one particular letter style to be followed for correspondence, generally the parts of a letter are positioned as follows.

Date: The date of a letter may appear in the center or near the right margin when the letter style used is either the Modified Block or Indented. When using the Extreme (or Full) Block style, the date appears on the far left, except when the letter is typed in a balanced Block style. For a balanced appearance, type the date directly across from the first line of the inside address and near the right margin. (See the sample letter in Figure 7-6.)

Inside Address: There are two positions for the inside address. One placement is below the date and the special notations (Confidential or Personal). The second placement follows all parts of the letter except the reference line. The Lower-Position inside address is used primarily when correspondence is of a formal or personal nature. On a letter such as those mentioned, the reference initials are typed below the address *on the file copy only.*

Attention Line: Type the attention line two spaces below the inside address at the left margin or centered.

Salutation: The salutation (or greeting) precedes the body of the letter and also the subject matter line, if there is one.

Re **or Subject Line:**   The subject matter of the letter is placed between the salutation and the body. Type the subject matter, following the Subject or *in re* caption, two spaces below the salutation. It may be centered or typed a few spaces to the right of the center. For an Extreme (or Full) Block letter, the subject matter line must begin at the left margin, the same as all parts of that letter. The subject matter line may be typed *to end* at the right margin if the letter is to take on the balanced Block look.

The Letter Body: This is the cluster of words and sentences that convey the message. The message may consist of one sentence, one paragraph, or several paragraphs and more than one page. The body follows the salutation.

The Complimentary Close: The complimentary close signifies the end of the message. The word or phrase is typed two spaces below the body of the letter near the center, unless it is the Extreme Block or balanced Block style. It is then typed at the far left.

Autograph: The handwritten signature should be placed *above* the typed signature.

Typed Signature: The typed signature position is four spaces below the complimentary close. If the person's name is printed on the letterhead, it is not necessary to type the name at the end of a letter, but it is not incorrect to do so, particularly if it is difficult to decipher the handwritten signature.

Reference Initials: The placement of the reference initials is usually at the left margin. The exception is the balanced Block style. The position is at the right margin.

The Postscript: The postscript follows two spaces below the last line of the letter which would be either the reference initials or the special mailing instructions. Type the dictator's initials at the close of the postscript.

Special Notations: Special notations are placed in chosen positions on the letterhead and the envelope. *Personal* and *Confidential* notations should be typed two spaces *above* the inside address. These words near the top of the letter will catch the reader's eye before the body of the letter is read, if the envelope is opened by mistake.

Mailing Instructions: Special mailing instructions (Air Mail, Special Delivery, etc.) should be typed below the reference initials and enclosure notations. The mailing instructions are the responsibility of the sender, not the receiver. With the reminder typed at the bottom of the letter, the secretary has an assembly-line type of outgoing mail operation.

Notations and Mailing Instructions on the Envelope: *Personal* and *Confidential* should be typed two spaces *above* the address on the envelope and slightly to the left. Some secretaries underline special notations and also the attention and subject matter line. Sometimes you will be told to mark the letter "Personal" after the letter has been signed and the envelope sealed. When this happens, mark the envelope "Personal" and type on the file copy of the letter that the envelope was so marked.

A notation such as "Hold for Arrival" should be typed in the bottom left-hand corner of the envelope.

The attention line generally is typed near the bottom of the envelope and to the far left.

Type the special mailing instructions where they will best serve the purpose. When mailing specifications require additional postage, type these notations below the area on the envelope where stamps and postage tape are to be affixed (Figure 7-1).

The Letter "Look."   Letters can easily be set up attractively if the typist will arrange the parts of the letter in suitable proportion to the letterhead design. Letterhead designs range from plain and small printing or engraving to decorative designs.

Using a letterhead design as the guide for setting up the letter, assume that the art work is two inches in depth spanning three-quarters the width of the paper and that the design clears the top of the sheet by one and a half inches. To balance the typed letter and the letterhead, the last line of the typed letter (reference initials or enclosure notation) should be approximately two

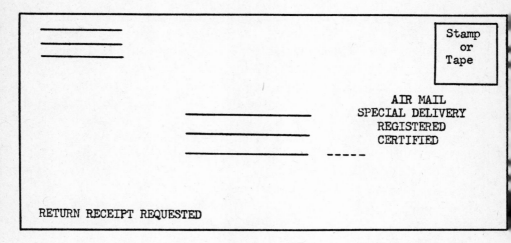

Figure 7-1. Placement of Mailing Instructions on Envelope.

inches from the bottom of the paper but not less than the distance between the top of the paper and the beginning of the letterhead design.

Left-hand and right-hand margins should be adjusted according to the length of the letter.

Use the *placement* of the design on the letterhead as a guide for the letter *style*. Select the style of letter that will complement the design. For example, the Extreme Block letter style may be the best one to use if the design center of interest is placed at the far right of the paper or if the art work is vertically spaced at the far right instead of spread across the top of the paper.

Business Letter Styles.   The following pages show the various styles of letters that cross the executive desk day in and day out (Figures 7-2 through 7-8).

Perhaps you are restricted to use one form only so that correspondence throughout the company will be uniform. Or, it may be a matter of choice in a smaller office, but one style can easily become the office style either because of speed and ease in typing it or because it appeals to your boss.

Some bosses enjoy having a letter presented for signature that has a different arrangement, but only if the message permits.

May 20, 19--

Messrs. Albert R. Times
    and James A. Times
TIMES JEWELRY COMPANY
230 North Dinley
Seattle, Washington 98111

Dear Messrs Times:

For the past six months we have been compiling facts and
figures that will help determine what hours of the working
day are the most productive in terms of dollar sales.

Information for this study was provided by our very own
sales representatives. Workday Record Sheets were completed by these representatives for a period of three
months.

Although sales are recorded from time to time by our other
employees, only those people who are classified as full
time sales people participated in this study.

After briefing our people on the purpose of the seemingly
tedious record-keeping task, their cooperation has enabled
us to draw some conclusions in the field of sales.

The results of this study are to be presented at the
annual convention of Those Who Sell, scheduled for the
first week in September.

Convention details and registration cards will be mailed
to you in approximately two months. Since we anticipate

Figure 7-2. Business Letter Style: Extreme Block, Two-Page Letter.

Messrs. Times
Page 2
May 20, 19--

a record convention attendance, this advance information
is to allow you to schedule your territorial sales visits
and make plans to register as many representatives as you
can spare.

Very truly yours,

INTERNATIONAL PRODUCTS

T. A. Duke
President

TAD:dat

Figure 7-2. Business Letter Style: Extreme Block, Two-Page Letter. (continued)

May 20, 19--

All Originals, Incorporated
1801 Market Avenue
Sherman, Texas   75090

Gentlemen:

      I am in the market for a water color painting
for my office. The predominant colors throughout the
office are blue and coral. The area where the painting
will hang is approximately 8' by 10'.

      Landscape or still life subjects would be
suitable. My plans are to be in Sherman next Monday
around noon. In the meantime, perhaps you can select
some color transparencies for viewing along with the
originals now on display.

                 Sincerely yours,

                 PAUL LAND COMPANY

                 David P. Paul
                 Secretary-Treasurer

DPP:ppd

Figure 7-3. Business Letter Style: Modified Block Indented Paragraphs.

                                        May 20, 19--

Dear Dr. Salls:

Last night's program was one of the most interesting
and educational presentations ever scheduled for our
members.   You can be sure you left an indelible
message with all of us.

On behalf of the entire group, a thunderous "thank you"
for sharing your thoughts with hundreds of spellbound
listeners.

                                Sincerely yours,

Dr. Winthrop Salls
3334 West Chestnut
Cinnamon Grove, California 93000

Figure 7-4. Business Letter Style: Modified Block Lower-Position Inside
Address.

May 20, 19--

Mr. and Mrs. Collin Hunter III
53906 Winter Way
Phoenix, Arizona 85000

Dear Mr. and Mrs. Hunter:

RE: TOUR NO. 534

All travel arrangements and hotel reservations have been
confirmed for your cruise scheduled for departure Monday,
July 15.

Three copies of the three-week itinerary are enclosed.
Please review the itinerary and report any changes to us
immediately.

A complete line of services is standard practice for
our agency. Should you require any additional services
prior to your departure, please do not hesitate to let
us know.

We wish you a happy time during your cruise and a most
pleasant memory of your tour when you return to Phoenix.

Sincerely yours,

SEA TRAVEL, INC.

Vice President/Tours

/bbt

Figure 7-5. Business Letter Style: Modified Block with *Re* Line.

O'Dell and Company   May 20, 19--
580 Stage Place
Roanoke, Virginia 24001

Gentlemen:

                     Subject: Commercial Rental, No. W42

The required documents for leasing the warehouse, as
classified above, have been prepared and processed.

The original and two copies of the lease are enclosed
for your signature. One carbon copy is to be retained
in your office; the other copy and the original lease
should be returned to us within ten days.

Rental checks will be forwarded to the stipulated de-
pository.

Very truly,

SOUTHERN REALTY

Clinton Stone   CS:tap
Agent   Enc. 3

Figure 7-6. Business Letter Style: Block with Right Margin Detail.

The date, reference initials and enclosure line placed at the right margin give
the letter a balanced look.

May 20, 19--

Borrowers Life Insurance Company
1002 Sanders Street, Suite 408
Boston, Massachusetts   02100

POLICYHOLDERS DIVISION

Gentlemen:

Re: Policy No. 391 92

The Loan Agreement form has been completed according to your instructions. Please mail the check to the address below.

Very truly yours,

Gerald B. Thomas

Gerald B. Thomas
Post Office Box 276
Casey, Iowa   50048

Enclosures: 2

Air Mail

Figure 7-7. Business Letter Style: Modified Block Double Spaced.
Paragraphs must be indented if the letter is double spaced.

May 20, 19--

Miss Norma Evans
    9741 East Skylark
        Fairbanks, Alaska 99701

Dear Miss Evans:

    Your application for summer employment has been
reviewed, and we are pleased to tell you that we would
like for you to come for a personal interview.

    Interviews are held every Thursday from 10 a.m.
to 4 p.m. in my office, located in the Round Room.

    Please write us as soon as you have selected
the date you plan to be in Wyoming so that we can
arrange to have our hostess meet your plane and drive
you from the airport to the Round Room.

    We are looking forward to your visit.

                    Sincerely yours,

                    THREE-SQUARE DUDE RANCH

                    James D. Charles
                    James D. Charles
                    Personnel Manager

/mol

Figure 7-8. Business Letter Style: Indented.

Addressing the Envelope. There are two styles for addressing envelopes, but the number of lines in the address varies. The style used must conform with that of the business letter. Three-line addresses should be doublespaced; four or more lines to the address may be single spaced.

The envelope for all letter styles except the indented letter should be typed in one of the two arrangements.

Mr. M. K. Murphy, President
MURPHY-KIMBALL-BARNS EXPORTS
8121 Southwind Street
Detroit, Michigan 48200

or

Mr. M. K. Murphy

8121 Southwind Street

Detroit, Michigan 48200

Lines of the address on the envelope in which an Indented letter will be mailed are to be aligned the same as the inside address on the letterhead.

Mr. James P. Mars
Vice President
TREE TOP TOGS
42 West Tennison
Dayton, Ohio 45400

or

Mr. James P. Mars

42 West Tennison

Dayton, Ohio 45400

Mail reaches its destination systematically. Reading up from the last line of the address the Post Office Department would spot these divisions: Zip Code, state, city, street or Post Office box number, suite or room number, and the name.

The lines of the address from name to zip code are typed in this order: Name of individual, official title, firm name, street address or Post Office box number (use either the street or box number but not both), city, state, and Zip Code.

Samples of addresses are shown below:

Mr. Adam Brook, President
CLOCKMAKERS, INCORPORATED
Post Office Box 000
Detroit, Michigan   48200

Mr. Calvin Hunt, Jr.
Manager/Regional Sales
NATIONAL FABRIC COMPANY
14 East 22nd Avenue
Houston, Texas   77000

Clayton Company

121 West Tenth Street

Evanston, Illinois   60200

Spell out Company, Corporation, Incorporated, Limited unless the word is abbreviated on the business letterhead.

Address the Correspondent Properly.   Secretaries are expected to know how to address all correspondents properly.

The chart listed here shows models of the written address and salutation for various academic, business, ecclesiastical, and governmental positions. Addresses for some of the professional people are also included.

Carbon Copy Notation.   Before you begin typing a letter, check the special notations in your shorthand pad. Carbon copy notations should be made at the beginning of a dictated letter. Be sure you have sufficient carbon copies for those individuals who are to receive a copy of the letter.

If you indicate the number of carbon copies that are to be typed and distributed at the beginning of the dictated letter, you won't gasp when you find that, after transcribing the letter, a notation at the end of the dictated letter indicated that you should have typed extra carbon copies.

FORMS OF WRITTEN ADDRESS AND SALUTATION
ACADEMIC

Position	Address	Salutation
Chancellor	Chancellor Paul Marshall University of Voters (Address)	Dear Chancellor Marshall:
(with doctorate)	Dr. Paul Marshall or Paul Marshall, Ph.D. Chancellor, University of Voters (Address)	Dear Dr. Marshall:
Dean	Dean James L. Brunner College of ( ) University of Voters (Address)	Dear Dean Brunner:
President	Mr. Frank L. Cooley President, Miner College (Address)	Dear President Cooley:
(with doctorate)	Dr. Frank L. Cooley or Frank L. Cooley, Ph. D. President, Miner College (Address)	Dear Dr. Cooley:
Professo.	Professor Thomas K. Ewing Department of ( ) Bernard Rains College (Address)	Dear Professor Ewing:
(with doctorate)	Dr. Thomas K. Ewing or Thomas K. Ewing, Ed. D. Department of ( ) Bernard Rains College (Address)	Dear Dr. Ewing:

FORMS OF WRITTEN ADDRESS AND SALUTATION (CONTINUED)

BUSINESS

Position	Address	Salutation
Executive	Mr. Kirk G. Garrett Executive Vice President Miner County State Bank (Address)	Dear Mr. Garrett:
Individual's name and position unknown	Miner County State Bank (Address)	Gentlemen:

NOTE: "Gentlemen" is the correct salutation to use in a letter with an attention line.

ECCLESIASTICAL: CATHOLIC

Archbishop	Most Reverend (full name) Archbishop of ( ) (Address)	Your Excellency:
Bishop	Most Reverend (full name) Bishop of ( ) (Address)	Your Excellency:
Cardinal	His Eminence (given name) Cardinal (surname) Archbishop of ( ) (Address)	Your Eminence:

Monsignor
 	
(according to his rank)
	Right Reverend Monsignor
	    (full name)
	        or
	Very Reverend Monsignor
	    (full name)
	(Address)
		Right Reverend Monsignor:
		
		Very Reverend Monsignor:

FORMS OF WRITTEN ADDRESS AND SALUTATION (CONTINUED)

Position	Address	Salutation
Mother	Mother (name), O.S.B.* (Address)	Dear Mother (name):
Pope	His Holiness Pope (name) (Address)	Your Holiness:
Priest	The Reverend (full name) (Address)	Dear Father (surname):
Sister	Sister (name) (Address)	Dear Sister (name):

JEWISH

Rabbi	Rabbi (full name) (Congregation) (Address)	Dear Rabbi (surname):

PROTESTANT

Bishop	The Right Reverend (full name) Bishop of ( ) (Address)	Right Reverend Sir:
Dean	The Very Reverend (full name) Dean of ( ) (Address)	Very Reverend Sir:
Minister	The Reverend (full name) (Address)	Dear Mr. (surname):

---

*Or whatever the initials of the order may be.

FORMS OF WRITTEN ADDRESS AND SALUTATION (CONTINUED)
GOVERNMENT

Position	Address	Salutation
Associate Justice	Mr. Justice (surname) The Supreme Court of the United States Washington, D.C. (Zip Code)	Dear Mr. Justice:
The Chief Justice	The Chief Justice of the United States The Supreme Court Washington, D.C. (Zip Code)	Dear Mr. Chief Justice:
Cabinet Members: *Attorney General*	Honorable (full name) Attorney General Washington, D.C. (Zip Code)	Dear Mr. Attorney General:
Postmaster General	Honorable (full name) Postmaster General Washington, D.C. (Zip Code)	Dear Mr. Postmaster General:

Secretary of Agriculture
Secretary of Commerce
Secretary of Defense
Secretary of Health,
  Education and Welfare
Secretary of Hous-
  ing and Urban
  Development
Secretary of Interior
Secretary of Labor
Secretary of State
Secretary of
  Transportation
Secretary of the
  Treasury
	Honorable (full name)
	Secretary of ( )
	Washington, D.C. (Zip Code)
		Dear Mr. (or Madam)
		  Secretary:

Councilman *(city)*	Mr. (full name) (Address)	Dear Mr. (surname):

FORMS OF WRITTEN ADDRESS AND SALUTATION (CONTINUED)

Position	Address	Salutation
Governor	Honorable (full name) Governor of (state) (Address)	Dear Governor (surname):
Lieutenant Governor	Honorable (full name) Lieutenant Governor of (state) (Address)	Dear Mr. (surname):
Mayor	Honorable (full name) Mayor of (city) (Address)	Dear Mayor (surname):
The President	The President The White House Washington, D.C. (Zip Code)	Mr. President:
Representative	Honorable (full name) House of Representatives Washington, D.C. (Zip Code)	Dear Mr. (or Mrs.) (surname):
Senator	Honorable (full name) United States Senate Washington, D.C. (Zip Code)	Dear Senator (surname): (the same for a woman)
The Vice President	The Vice President United States Senate Washington, D.C. (Zip Code)	Mr. Vice President:

PROFESSIONAL

Dentist	Douglas I. Hill, D.D.S. *or* Dr. Douglas I Hill	All salutations would be Dear Dr. (surname):

FORMS OF WRITTEN ADDRESS AND SALUTATION (CONTINUED)

Position	Address	Salutation
Optometrist	Richard Stills, O.D. *or* Dr. Richard Stills	
Physician/Surgeon	Kenneth Vase, M.D. *or* Dr. Kenneth Vase	
Veterinarian	R. L. Orange, D.V.M. *or* Dr. R. L. Orange	

NOTE: Do not add any title to the first form of address. A woman would be addressed as Ann Crane, M.D. or Dr. Ann Crane. Socially she would be addressed Mrs. B. O. Crane.

Unless it is to be a blind carbon copy notation, type the names of the people who are to receive a copy. Prior to distributing the carbon copies, place a check mark following the person's name, to designate the carbon copy intended for him.

The carbon copy notation and the person designated to receive the copy will appear as in Figure 7-9.

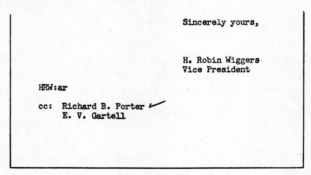

Figure 7-9. Carbon Copy Notation.

Blind Carbon Copy Notation.   It may not be necessary for the recipient of the original letter to know that a carbon copy of that letter has been routed to some other person; but your records must always be a source of correct and complete information. Therefore, the blind carbon copy notation must be typed on the *carbon copies only*. The blind carbon copy notation should appear on the copy you retain for your file, and it should also appear on the carbon copy that is sent to the designated person.

The person who is to receive the carbon copy of the letter must be aware of the fact that the addressee does not know that he is to receive a carbon copy of the letter; otherwise, a blind carbon copy notation on the file copy only may not adequately serve the purpose for which it was intended.

An example of a blind carbon copy notation is shown in Figure 7-10.

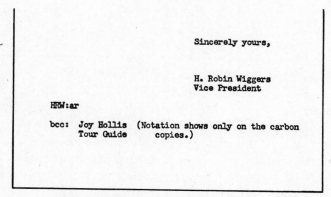

Figure 7-10. Blind Carbon Copy Notation.

Penned Postscripts. When your boss pens a postscript at the bottom of the typewritten letter, read it. If it pertains in any way to the business or if there is the slightest chance it will draw response from the recipient, type the penned comments on the file copy of the letter. Make a notation, too, that the postscript was handwritten on the original letter. This is your record; and it will be helpful if there is further comment about the penned postscript.

Mailing Instructions. Indicate at the end of the transcribed letter any special mail service the letter is to receive from your office. If you are instructed to send a letter via Air Mail service, make this notation on the letter.

Figure 7-11 shows the specific mailing instruction.

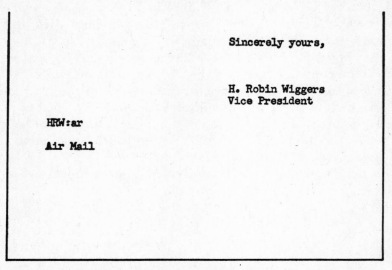

Figure 7-11. Mail Instruction Placement on Letter.

Enclosure and Special Mail Notation.   Sometimes letters are to be certified or registered through the post office. At the end of the letter, make a notation of any special mail service. Show also that a return receipt card has been requested, if this is the case.

Figure 7-12 indicates that an enclosure was mailed with the

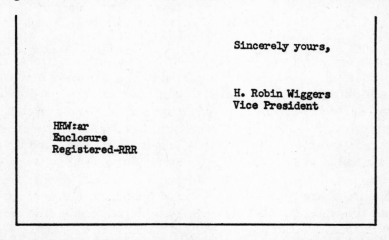

Figure 7-12. Enclosure Notation and Mail Instruction Placement on Letter.

letter and that the letter was registered and a return receipt card was requested.

Personal or Confidential Notation.   Personal letters and confidential letters should be so marked.

On the envelope, the words "Confidential" or "Personal" should be typed above and several spaces to the left of the name of the individual to whom the letter is addressed.

For future reference, or as a record that a special notation was made on the envelope, type a note to this effect on the *carbon copy* only of the letter.

Figure 7-13 is an example of such a notation.

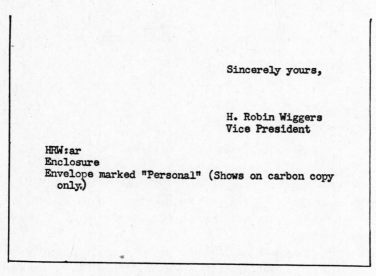

```
                              Sincerely yours,



                              H. Robin Wiggers
                              Vice President

HRW:ar
Enclosure
Envelope marked "Personal" (Shows on carbon copy
   only.)
```

Figure 7-13. "Personal" Notation.

Letters Delivered in Person.   Your boss may ask you to type a letter that is not intended for mailing but which will be delivered personally to the addressee. This may happen when the two individuals, your boss and the addressee, have arranged to meet at a particular place or in another city, and time does not allow for mailing the letter prior to the scheduled meeting.

For the record, indicate this special action on the carbon copy of the letter.

Figure 7-14 shows the notation made on the *carbon copy* of a letter when the original is being delivered to the addressee personally.

```
                                      Sincerely yours,


                                      H. Robin Wiggers
                                      Vice President

HRW:ar
Enclosure

Note:  Original letter to be delivered in person by
       Mr. Adamson at real estate meeting in Omaha
       tomorrow (3-2-65).
```

Figure 7-14. Letter Delivered in Person Notation.

Enclosures Should Be Described.   Just to indicate at the end of a letter that enclosures were mailed along with the letter may not be sufficient when the time comes to recall exactly what the enclosures were.

Following the notation, "Enclosures," type in parentheses the number of papers that are enclosed in a letter, *if the enclosures are described* in the body of the letter.

Figure 7-15 describes the material that is being enclosed with the letter.

Enclosures that are not described in the body of the letter should be briefly described at the end of the letter, following the word "Enclosures."

A brief notation at the end of a letter describing enclosures not described in the body of the letter will be an aid when time has passed and you have no other way of knowing what documents were enclosed with the letter.

The sample letter in Figure 7-16 shows this notation.

(LETTER DESCRIBING ENCLOSURES)

Dear Harris:

Your interest in the proposed plan for developing the twenty acres has encouraged me to continue the project.

To complete the first legal requirement, I'm sending you a map of the area and four drawings of the buildings to be erected on the specified locations.

You may now proceed in the manner discussed yesterday.

Sincerely yours,

PJA:ar
Enclosures (5)

Figure 7-15. Enclosure Description.

(ENCLOSURES NOT DESCRIBED IN BODY OF LETTER)

Dear Harris:

Your interest in my proposed plan to develop the acreage has certainly encouraged me to continue.

So that requirements will be met by the first of October, I'm sending you some material pertinent to the plan. I'll discuss this with you next week.

Sincerely yours,

PJA:ar

Enclosures: Map of Section 3, Twp. 14S, Rge. 48E, Peacock County; Four drawings--House A, House B, House C and House D.

Figure 7-16. Enclosure Description.

Enclosure Attached to Carbon Copy for Another to Process. It may be necessary to inform more than one other employee of specific business transactions.

Your boss may answer a letter containing an enclosure which is ordinarily handled in another department; but because the letter was addressed for your boss' personal attention, he acknowledges the letter. However, he would want the proper processing department personnel to know about the transaction. The procedure might be to send a carbon copy of your boss' answering

(ENCLOSURE INTENDED FOR ANOTHER
DEPARTMENT)

Dear Mr. Tidings:

　　　　Last night we rushed our son to the hospital for emergency treatment. He was climbing, lost his footing--consequently, he needed special treatment.

　　　　We're still newcomers in your city, but I remember the speech you gave a couple week's ago at the Weekenders' Club, and also remembered that you are the hospital administrator.

　　　　I apologize for taking up your time, but I would appreciate your channeling this check, in payment of last night's emergency, to the proper individual.

　　　　I look forward to sharing another luncheon with you as guest speaker in the near future.

　　　　　　　Sincerely,

　　　　　　　Ben Derrick

Enc. (Check No. 32)

Figure 7-17. Enclosure Intended for Another Department.

letter, with the enclosure attached, to the personnel that would ordinarily handle the request which was directed to your boss.

For example, if the enclosure is customarily handled by the insurance clerk, your boss will indicate that he is to receive a copy of the letter and the enclosure. The letter in Figure 7-17 indicates that a check was sent to your boss, in payment of services. The check is handled by the insurance clerk.

Your boss' reply to the foregoing letter might be similar to the one in Figure 7-18.

(LETTER ACKNOWLEDGING ENCLOSURE INTENDED
FOR ANOTHER DEPARTMENT)

Dear Mr. Derrick:

Your son's accident very vividly reminded me of our first weekend, as newcomers, in this city. It must be some sort of "official initiation," and I welcome you to a fine community.

I will personally see to it that your check reaches the Insurance Clerk. Hope your son is rapidly mending so that he can enjoy the beautiful countryside.

I drive by your office on my way to the Weekenders' Club meetings. May I pick you up Tuesday? I'll call you at your office early Tuesday morning.

Sincerely yours,

Kevin Tidings

KT:jt
cc: Insurance Clerk w/check
        No. 32 ($35.00)

Figure 7-18.

Note also that your boss' reply letter contains an obligation incurred by your boss—a telephone call to Mr. Derrick early Tuesday morning. Make a notation on both your boss' calendar and your calendar that he is to telephone Mr. Derrick Tuesday morning and provide the transportation to the meeting mentioned. Perhaps your boss will welcome a verbal reminder on the morning of the meeting that his schedule will include the telephone call and the drive to the invited passenger's office.

Additional Pages of a Letter. Headings for the second and additional pages of a letter should include the name of the addressee, the date, and the page number. The heading alignment many times is a matter of choice. Some companies may, for uniformity, specify that additional page headings follow an established pattern.

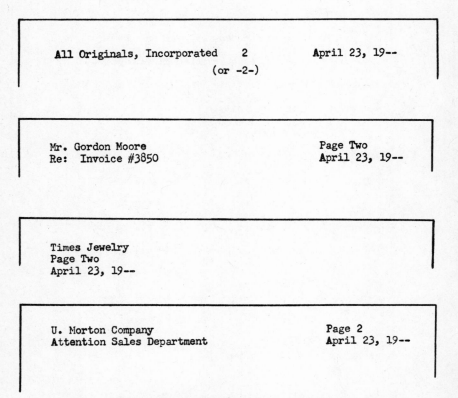

Figure 7-19. Multiple-Page Letter Headings.

Various headings for additional pages of letters are shown in Figure 7-19.

The firm name and the signature should be typed on the last page of a letter when the letter consists of more than one page. It is possible that the first page of a letter could become separated from additional pages; if the firm name and signature do not appear on the last page, it may take a good deal of time to find the page mate.

Figure 7-20 is an example of what the last page of a letter should show, in addition to the page heading.

```
                                    Sincerely yours,

                                    SPENCELEY COMPANY



                                    Thomas Spenceley, III
                                    Regional Manager/Sales

        TS,III/cf
```

Figure 7-20. Multiple-Page Letter Signature Box.

8

Mailing Tips

Incoming mail is usually answered during the regular workday, just as a majority of incoming telephone calls are returned during office hours.

The suggestions and mail tips in this chapter may be an inducement to handle the outgoing mail with the same speed and concern as other office duties are handled.

Sort and Band the Mail. Sort the outgoing mail into stacks: Local, Out of Town, and Air Mail. Band these stacks separately.

Use your mail tray as a sorter. Draw an imaginery line down the center of your mail tray. Place local mail on one side and out-of-town mail on the other side of the imaginery line. Do this every day. When it's time to band the mail, sorting has already been done.

Mailing Staples and Paper Clips. Whenever a staple will easily puncture and securely hold related papers to be mailed, do not use a paper clip, particularly in envelopes Size 10 or smaller.

Over-stuffed Envelopes. Don't stuff an envelope beyond its holding capacity. Keep a supply of various sizes of envelopes on hand and use one that is strong enough and large enough to hold the material to be mailed.

Hint for Applying Postage to Thick Envelopes. Occasionally the thickness of large envelopes such as 9x12 makes it necessary to use postage meter tape instead of using only the postage meter for the amount of postage that is required for mailing the envelope.

How do you affix the correct amount of postage on a thick envelope when there is no tape in the postage meter and a new roll of tape is not at hand so that you could feed the tape into the machine? Solve the problem by following the steps listed:

1. Weigh the envelope and its contents *without sealing the envelope* (or merely place the papers on top of the envelope and weigh).
2. Remove the papers from the envelope.
3. Fold the envelope to a width that will go through the mailing machine letter guide.
4. Set the postage meter for the correct amount of postage and guide the folded envelope through the mailing machine so that the meter will print the postage directly onto the envelope.
5. Insert the papers into the envelope, seal, and mail.

Air Mail Letters.   Send letters mailed by Air early on Thursdays only if the destination office is open on Saturdays and distance would make delivery possible; otherwise, send letters on Thursdays and Fridays First Class.

Volume Mail.   Occasionally, or regularly, perhaps, your office sends out thousands of letters or statements. Inform your local post office that you are preparing a large mailing list so that they can prepare for the volume mail.

Check with the post office for service available whereby your mail can be picked up early in the day.

Machine Sealed Envelopes.   When regular postage stamps are used for a large mailing list, you can save time sealing the envelopes by setting the mailing machine postage meter for sealing purposes only. A postage mark will not appear if the machine is set in this manner.

Hand-Applied Postage Stamps.   Before affixing postage stamps, fold the stamps back and forth at the perforations. This makes separating easy and quick; and it should eliminate tearing a stamp in two. Fold several rows of stamps back and forth at one time.

Postdate for Morning Delivery or Pickup.   Statements and periodic mailings can be postdated and mailed on the morning of the corresponding date.

The following information was supplied for reproduction by Customer Relations, United States Post Office, Denver, Colorado:

● Airmail stamps and envelopes are for AIRMAIL only. (The use of one airmail stamp with regular postage makes the mailing piece liable for air postage. Likewise, airmail envelopes must carry airmail rate postage.)

● Objects such as coins, keys, trinkets, jewelry, bottle caps, etc. are nonmailable in *envelopes;* they should be prepared in package form.

● Third-class matter in *sealed* envelopes or packages must be endorsed "Third Class"; otherwise first-class postage will be charged.

● Certified mail is for the United States and its possessions *only.* It does not provide insurance coverage. A delivery record is kept.

● Special delivery stamps are good for special delivery service *only.*

● Corner addresses, such as 16th & Curtis, or Alameda & University Blvd. should NOT be used. Definite street numbers are assigned to each location by City Engineers and should be used.

● A complete address should be used in all cases for efficient mail service—name, number and street or post office box number, city, state, and ZIP Code. If the address is to a building or an apartment house, then the room, suite, or apartment number must follow the number and street in the address. A building name should not be used as an address.

● After 4 p.m., hold your routine mailings (notices, statements, and other mail of no urgency) for the next-morning pickup. Postdate meter mail for a current date. This clears the way for the speedy dispatch of your later afternoon letters—the ones where quick delivery really matters.

● Early mailing should be *your* concern, no matter how few or how many letters.

PREPARATION OF METERED MAIL

● Meter stamps must be legible and not overlap. Illegible or overlapping stamps will not be considered as valid postage.

• When metered stamps are printed on tape, only tape approved by the Post Office Department may be used.

• Metered stamps must be printed or stuck on the upper right corner of the envelope, address label, or tag.

• Meter stamps must show city, state, meter number, and amount of postage on all classes of mail. When additional tapes or stamps are used, the circle showing the post office must appear on each (Figure 8-1).

• Meter stamps must show the date of mailing on all of the following: *First-class, special delivery, special handling, air mail, registered, insured, and COD's.* The *month* and *year must* be shown on tapes on second-, third-, or fourth-class mail, but the day may be omitted. When the meter impression is imprinted *directly on* second- or third-class mail, the date must not be shown.

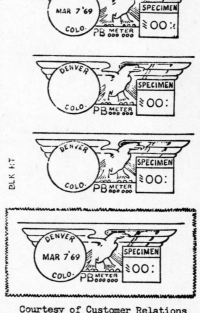

FIRST CLASS

Always show Date, City and State

THIRD CLASS

OMIT Date. Show City and State

BULK THIRD CLASS

OMIT Date. Show City, State and
Bulk Legend

ON TAPE OR ADDRESS LABELS - ALL CLASSES

Always show Date, City and State
(The Day may be omitted on ordinary
2nd, 3rd and 4th class mail)

Courtesy of Customer Relations
United States Post Office
Denver, Colorado   80202

Figure 8-1. Postage Meter Designs.

● Metered mail must be faced with addresses in the same direction and securely tied in bundles. Special delivery and air mail should be bundled separately; if only a few pieces, place them on top of the bundle.

● Do not mix first- and third-class mail in the same bundle or in the same sack as delay might result to the first-class mail. Don't mix metered mail and mail with postage stamps affixed.

● The postage meter *DATE must be current when mail is received in the Post Office.* Any mail deposited in a collection box that has been collected for the last time daily (check collection box schedule) must be post-dated for a current date when the mail is collected the following day.

SPECIAL MAIL SERVICES*

REGISTERED MAIL

WHY   [Mail is registered as an] added protection for valuable and important mail and evidence of mailing and delivery may be obtained by having it registered.

WHAT   All mailable matter prepaid with postage at the first-class or airmail rate may be registered. Stamps or meter stamps must be attached to the mail representing all postage and fee charges. Business reply mail may not be registered unless postage and all fees are fully prepaid.

VALUE   The sender is required by law to tell the postal clerk, or to enter on the firm mailing bill if a firm mailer, the FULL value of mail matter presented for registration. The fact that private insurance may be carried on registered mail does not modify the requirement for declaring the value as defined below:

---

*Information pertaining to special mail services and Zip Coding courtesy Post Office Department, Washington, D.C.

Kind of Mail Matter	Value to Be Declared
Negotiable instruments—Instruments payable to bearer, and MATURED interest coupons.	Market value.
Nonnegotiable instruments—All registered bonds, warehouse receipts, checks, drafts, deeds, wills, abstracts, and similar documents. Certificates of stock, including those endorsed in blank, are considered nonnegotiable so far as declaration of value is concerned.	No value, or replacement cost if postal insurance coverage is desired.
Money -	Full value.
Jewelry, gems, precious metals - - - -	Market value or cost.
Merchandise - - - - - - - - - - - - - - -	Market value or cost.
Nonvaluables—matter not having intrinsic value such as letters, files, records, etc.	No value, or replacement cost if postal insurance coverage is desired.

ADDITIONAL SERVICES

There is an extra fee for these additional services:

COD

Restricted Delivery

Return Receipts:
    Requested at time of mailing:
        Showing to whom and when delivered
        Showing to whom, when, and address where delivered
    Requested after mailing:
        Showing to whom and when delivered

CERTIFIED MAIL

Certified mail service provides for a receipt to the sender and a record of delivery at the office of address. No record is kept at the office at which mailed. It is handled in the ordinary mail and no insurance coverage is provided. The mail will be endorsed as shown in Figure 8-2.

Figure 8-2.

Any mailable matter of no intrinsic value on which postage at the first-class rate has been paid will be accepted as certified mail. This does not exclude articles of a nonnegotiable character and other similar matter which would involve a cost of duplication if lost or destroyed. The mail may be sent by air on payment of the required postage. Special delivery services are available on payment of the prescribed fees. Penalty and franked mail may be accepted as certified mail if the fee is prepaid. . . . Business reply mail must be fully prepaid with postage and fees.

FEES

The fee for certified mail is in addition to postage, as are the following additional services fees:

> Restricted Delivery
> Return Receipts:
>   Requested at time of mailing:
>   Showing to whom and date delivered
>   Showing to whom, date, and address where delivered
>   Requested after mailing.
>   Showing to whom and date delivered

The fee and postage may be paid by ordinary postage stamps, meter stamps, or by permit imprints.

ZIP CODE

ZIP Code [Zoning Improvement Plan] is a five-digit geographic code that identifies areas within the United States and its possessions for purposes of simplifying the distribution of mail by the U. S. Post Office Department. It should appear on the last line of both the destination and return addresses of mail following the names of city and State.

The Post Office Department has authorized the following 2 letter State and other abbreviations to help volume mailers make room for ZIP Codes in existing addressing systems (Figure 8-3).

Alabama	AL	Montana	MT
Alaska	AK	Nebraska	NB
Arizona	AZ	Nevada	NV
Arkansas	AR	New Hampshire	NH
California	CA	New Jersey	NJ
Colorado	CO	New Mexico	NM
Connecticut	CT	New York	NY
Delaware	DE	North Carolina	NC
District of Columbia	DC	North Dakota	ND
Florida	FL	Ohio	OH
Georgia	GA	Oklahoma	OK
Guam	GU	Oregon	OR
Hawaii	HI	Pennsylvania	PA
Idaho	ID	Puerto Rico	PR
Illinois	IL	Rhode Island	RI
Indiana	IN	South Carolina	SC
Iowa	IA	South Dakota	SD
Kansas	KS	Tennessee	TN
Kentucky	KY	Texas	TX
Louisiana	LA	Utah	UT
Maine	ME	Vermont	VT
Maryland	MD	Virginia	VA
Massachusetts	MA	Virgin Islands	VI
Michigan	MI	Washington	WA
Minnesota	MN	West Virginia	WV
Mississippi	MS	Wisconsin	WI
Missouri	MO	Wyoming	WY

Figure 8-3. Authorized Two-Letter Abbreviations of States, etc.

CHECKLIST FOR OUTGOING MAIL

Find out what time the mail clerk arrives at your office to pick up mail that is to be readied for the post office. Help the mail clerk maintain a schedule. Sort and band your mail that has been stamped and sealed and is ready for delivery to the post office.

Mailing Instructions.   Letters that are to be sent Air Mail, Special Delivery, Registered, Certified, etc. should be inserted in envelopes with such a marking. In order to be sure that you won't forget to indicate on the envelope the type of mail service the letter is to receive, type the envelope before transcribing the letter.

Foreign Rates.   The rate may vary for mail sent to foreign countries. Failure to affix the correct amount of postage may be cause for the letter to be returned to your office for additional postage. Time is lost by this oversight.

Omitting the Cover Letter.   Your boss may instruct you to mail a packet of the company's promotional material to an individual he met on a trip, but he does not dictate a letter, nor does he enclose a handwritten note.

Make a list of the printed material you are sending to the addressee. On the sheet with the list of material to be mailed, show the date the material was mailed, the name, and the complete mailing address. (You might also type a note on the sheet to identify the individual, such as where your boss met him and what his business interest is.)

Before mailing a publication which is of special interest to the receiver, outline the article or fasten a signal to the page on which the article appears for quick reference.

Enclosures.   Enclosures should be secured to the letter with a staple instead of using a paper clip for this purpose.

Reminder

Any enclosure not described in the body of the letter should be described at the end of the letter, following the word, "Enclosure."

The Signature Makes It Official.   The letters that your boss dictated to you should also bear his signature.

It won't happen often, but it does happen, that one letter may be returned to your desk without your boss' signature. Check "signed" letters for missing signatures. Check the letters for proper *signature placement,* also.

9

Business Writing Made Easy

This chapter is a brief review of punctuation, spelling, word division, capitalization, numbers as words and as figures, and abbreviations.

PUNCTUATION

Punctuate the material dictated to you and your own compositions so that the message is interpreted as intended.

Apostrophe (')

1. Use the apostrophe to show possession (Ownership):

    The firm's earnings increased by 3.4%.
    Mail the consignor's copy to him.
    This rack is for men's coats.
    Do you hear children's voices?

The above examples show that 's is added to singular nouns and also to plural nouns that do not end in s.
Add only the apostrophe to plural nouns that end in s:

    That is our bosses' parking area.
    She will receive ten days' pay.
    Several university students' cars were in the parade.

Do *not* use the apostrophe with definite possessive pronouns, which are written with all letters joined:

His, hers, theirs, ours, its, yours.

Add *'s* to form the possessive case of indefinite pronouns:

Someone's, anybody's, everybody's

2. Use the apostrophe to form contractions:

> *Would not* becomes wouldn't
> *Was not* becomes wasn't
> *It is* becomes it's

3. Use the apostrophe to indicate that letters or numbers have been omitted:

> S'prise!
> Crop records for the '40s and '50s are being compared with current production.

4. Use an apostrophe to show measurement in minutes:

> ... thence south 40° 20' (minutes) along the South line, a distance of 278 feet.

5. Use an apostrophe to form the plural of abbreviations with periods and to eliminate confusion when letters are used as nouns:

B.F.A.'s, U's, a's

Asterisk (*)

1. Use an asterisk as a footnote reference in tables consisting of numerals:

Maintenance
and Repairs
$12,387*

---

*This amount does not include the new unit purchased last week.

2. Use asterisks as a substitute for an unprintable word:

> He said excitedly, "We really had to work—that was *** tough
> competition!"

Brackets [ ]

1. Material quoted in error and comments added to the original
material are to be enclosed in brackets:

> ". . . one small step for [a] man, one giant leap for mankind."

2. Parenthetical material within parentheses should be boxed
with brackets:

> Personal knowledge (the truth [contrary to voiced and published
> opinions]) is this: The original painting was not framed.

Colon (:)

1. Use the colon to indicate additional material follows:

> Keep the following items handy: shorthand pads, pencils, erasers,
> carbon paper, and letterhead.
> To Wit: Beginning at the Northeast Quarter Corner, thence east,
> a distance of fifty feet along the East line . . .

2. Use a colon to mark the end of the salutation:

> Dear Mr. Merchant: Mr. President:

3. Use a colon to introduce a long quotation:

> His report began: "Many vehicles travel this highway daily. South-
> bound traffic alone is estimated to be between 54,200 and
> 55,000 cars and trucks each day."

4. Use a colon to separate hours and minutes when time is
reported in figures:

> The meeting began at 10:15 a.m.

Comma (,)

1. Use a comma to separate a series of words:

> That was a loud, strange, and frightening noise.

2. Use a comma to separate independent (also known as main or co-ordinate) clauses joined by a conjunction. (Independent clauses can stand alone as complete sentences—each has a subject and a verb.)

> The carnival was considered the most enjoyable event of the school
>   year, and a similar program is being planned for next year.
> Thomas graduates in two years, but he hasn't decided where he will
>   set up his legal practice.
> The drive through the mountains was a pleasant one, and the cool
>   nights were most enjoyable.

3. Use a comma to separate subordinate elements such as nonrestrictive clauses and phrases from an independent clause:

> Because it snowed during the night, he shoveled the sidewalk.
> Although machinery is available which would increase production,
>   he prefers to do the carving by hand.
> Having fluctuated during the day, the market closed steady.

However, do not separate a restrictive element from the main clause. (A restrictive element is any clause or phrase used in addition to the main clause and by its omission it would change the basic intent of the sentence, thus no commas.)

> RESTRICTIVE: Mr. Evans' file which contains a complete record of
>   his personal accounts must be examined.
> NONRESTRICTIVE: Mr. Evans' accounts, which have been filed in
>   our office for a number of years, must be examined.
> RESTRICTIVE: The price that is listed in the catalog is $7.95 plus
>   postage and handling.
> NONRESTRICTIVE: The price is $7.95, including postage and
>   handling.

4. Use a comma to set off a subordinate element from an independent clause when the subordinate element begins the sentence:

After she typed the report, Catherine gathered information for her
    next assignment.
As soon as the judging was completed, the winner was announced.

If the subordinate element follows the independent clause, the
two are not separated by a comma:

The birds began to chirp as soon as the rain stopped.
The winner was announced immediately following the judging.

5. Use a comma to set off an identifying word or phrase from
the rest of the sentence:

Miss Wilson, the design coordinator, will be here next week.
Mr. Adams, the vice president, has been with the company twenty-
    five years.
Our sales representative, Hugh Andrews, will be in your area in
    June.

6. Use a comma to separate parenthetical expressions from the
rest of the sentence:

He made no attempt, however, to solicit votes.
Quality, indeed, is important.
This plan, we believe, is the most feasible one.
Robert, I understand, will vacation in South America for three
    weeks.
The bulletin, by the way, is on the board.

Parenthetical expressions are words or phrases that are not
necessary in conveying the message.
7. Use a comma to separate the city from the state in sentences
and address lines:

The convention will be held in Miami, Florida next spring.

Mr. J. A. Crane
1476 Tenth Street
Portland, Oregon 97200

8. Use a comma to separate the day from the year:

His birthdate is August 21, 1939.

9. Use a comma to set off direct quotations:

Helen asked, "Is that an antique?"
Kenneth answered, "Yes, it is."

10. Use a comma to set off introductory words and a direct address:

Yes, payment is due when merchandise is delivered.
Mr. Hale, your appointment for Friday has been confirmed.
The lawn, Marge, must be manicured.

11. Do not use a comma to set off fragments of quoted material:

He said a "reasonable amount" would open the bidding.
The new schedule is described as "highly effective."

Dash (−)

The dash is made by striking the hyphen twice. It is not separated from the end of the preceding word or the beginning of the following word.
1. Use a dash for emphasis or to stress a point:

The evenings are cool—bring a warm jacket or sweater.
The lesson today will be on the primary colors—red, yellow, and
    blue.

2. Use a dash to indicate an abrupt change in thought:

Skiing was fun—just great—last weekend.
Those low temperatures—five degrees below zero—kept us inside.

Ellipsis (. . .)

An ellipsis is used when words have been omitted from quoted material.
A three-spaced ellipsis shows that material within a sentence has been omitted:

It has been the policy of this company to develop . . . effective
    methods.

The four-spaced ellipsis shows that the last part of the sentence was not quoted:

> Many of the suggestions for improvements were considered at the conference. . . .

Exclamation Mark (!)

1. Use the exclamation mark to carry the writer's emotion to the reader:

> That's wonderful! Congratulations!

2. Use the exclamation mark to emphasize a point:

> That is a fact! It really works!

Hyphen (-)

1. Use a hyphen with compound numbers when written as words:

> He is twenty-one years old.
> Forty-nine people attended the recital.
> One hundred thirty-two applications were reviewed last month.

2. Use a hyphen with one-thought modifiers preceding a noun:

> There is a ready-to-wear shop two blocks from here.
> *But:* The dress is ready to wear.
> He is leaving shortly to attend an out-of-town meeting.
> *But:* The meeting is out of town.

3. Use a hyphen when several adjectives are carried through a sentence by one base word modifying the same noun:

> Short-, intermediate-, and long-term changes are being studied.

Parentheses ( )

1. Use parentheses to enclose one or several words that will not

change the main thought in the sentence. The material enclosed in parentheses would be additional information or an explanation:

> Mark your answers either True (T) or False (F).
> On the line following each word in the list, write the correct tense (Past, Present, or Future).
> The illustration (Figure 21) can be adapted to your own use.

2. Use parentheses following amounts or numbers written as words:

> The loan value of the policy is One Hundred Forty-six Dollars ($146), and it is to be repaid in multiples of no less than Ten Dollars ($10).
> This notice is to be published consecutively for six (6) days.

3. Use parentheses to enclose numbers or letters that identify items in a list:

> As you reread your papers, check for these possible errors: (1) misspelled words, (2) incorrect spacing, and (3) double impressions.
> Employee rating sheets cover the following:
> (a) Promptness
> (b) Personal appearance
> (c) Accuracy
> (d) Attitude

Period (.)

1. Use a period with accepted abbreviations:

> Mr.   Dr.   10:34 p.m.   U.S. Highway 30

2. Use a period to end a declarative sentence (a statement of fact or condition) and to end an imperative sentence (a command or polite request).

> *Declarative:* Bradley leaves for work at six in the morning.
> Six students were selected for the special experiment.
> *Imperative:* Lock the door.
> Please enclose payment for the balance due on your account.

Question Mark (?)

1. Use a question mark at the end of an interrogative sentence (a sentence that asks a question):

> How many fish did you catch before noon?
> Who is playing the violin?

2. Use a question mark to indicate doubt:

> They climbed the mountain in twelve (?) hours.
> He said that he can drive forty (?) miles on one gallon of gas.

Single Quotation Marks (' ')

Use single quotation marks to set off quoted material within a quotation. The direct quotation begins with double (") quotation marks:

> Before the game, the coach said: "This game is anticipated to be
> tough, but 'It isn't whether we win or lose but how we play the
> game.' "

Quotation Marks (" ")

1. Use quotation marks to enclose the exact words of a speaker or author:

> "You must remember," he said, "that distance was a factor."
> She asked, "How many copies shall I make?"
> He answered, "Type three carbon copies."
> James shouted, "Close the window!"
> What did he mean when he said, "See you next week"?

Periods and commas are placed inside quotation marks.

The question mark is placed inside quotation marks when the quotation is a question. When the quoted material is not a question, the question mark follows the quotation marks.

The same placement applies to an exclamation mark. If the quotation draws an exclamatory response from the person quoting the source, the exclamation mark must be placed outside the quotation marks.

2. Use one set of quotation marks to indicate measurement in seconds:

> . . . thence south 20° 20' 30" (seconds) along the South line to the point of beginning.

Semicolon (;)

1. Use a semicolon to separate independent clauses when they are not connected by a co-ordinate conjunction:

> Most of the "ranch family" went to the picnic on horseback; four of us went by car to meet them.
> The system is very effective; it cuts down the production time by 15% thereby reducing cost.

2. Use a semicolon to separate compound sentences connected by an adverb (inasmuch, therefore, however, namely):

> The forecast calls for rain; nevertheless, campers are to meet as planned.
> She aspires to a career in the theatre; consequently, she insists that acting and drama are necessary courses of study.
> Sale items are to be reduced according to stock; however, no reduction is to exceed 50% of the retail price.

3. Use a semicolon when commas are used within a series:

> The days and dates of the show are as follows: Wednesday, December 5; Friday, December 7; and Saturday, December 8.
> Evans County had four blue ribbon winners; Bailey County had three winners, one blue and two red ribbons; and Manner County had five white ribbon winners.

Place the semicolon outside quotation marks:

> These are the topics for tonight's program: "Away from Harvest"; "Yesterday and Tomorrow"; and "Are 'Future' and 'Infinity' the Same?"

SPELLING

Sometimes the misspelling of a word should be counted as a typographical error instead of a "spelling" error; therefore, the following list includes words that may be a spelling or a typing problem.

1. abroad	26. government
2. academic	27. harass
3. accessible	28. imperative
4. accommodate	29. inadvertently
5. accumulate	30. initiative
6. amateur	31. itinerary
7. attendant	32. lien
8. baccalaureate	33. lieu
9. barrage	34. maneuver
10. bulletin	35. miniature
11. calendar	36. numerical
12. canvas (cloth)	37. occasionally
13. canvass (solicit)	38. omitted
14. clause	39. parallel
15. conscience	40. privilege
16. conscious	41. proportion
17. criticize	42. recipient
18. column	43. relevant
19. deterrent	44. similar
20. ecclesiastical	45. specifically
21. etiquette	46. stationary (fixed position)
22. exorbitant	47. stationery (paper)
23. familiar	48. triple
24. fulfill	49. unanimous
25. foreign	50. vacuum

The above words were checked for correct spelling in *Webster's Seventh New Collegiate Dictionary*.

RULES OF SPELLING

The first rule for spelling in the office: Never guess, use the dictionary.

WORD DIVISION

Prefixes

When a prefix and a root word become a new word, it is written as a solid word. There are exceptions.

Prefix	Root Word	Spelling
semi	annual	semiannual
sub	standard	substandard
un	skilled	unskilled
hyper	sensitive	hypersensitive
over	lap	overlap
dis	courage	discourage
under	nourished	undernourished
post	date	postdate

EXCEPTIONS

1. Hyphenate words that have identical spellings but different meanings:

re-creation — created again
recreation — leisure time

re-lease — to lease again
release — set free

2. Hyphenate *ex* when it denotes former status:

ex-mayor
ex-hunter
ex-Virginian

3. Hyphenate words when adding the prefix *self:*

self-addressed
self-denial
self-respect

4. Hyphenate a prefix and captialized word:

mid-Atlantic
pro-American
pre-Columbian

Suffixes

When the last letter of the word is a silent *e* and the suffix begins with a consonant, retain the *e* and add the suffix:

productiveness   timeless
respectively   procurement

EXCEPTIONS:

truly
awful
judgment

When the last letter of the word is a silent *e* and the suffix begins with a vowel drop the *e* and add the suffix:

typewriting
encouraging
endurance
acceleration

EXCEPTIONS:

mileage
chargeable
advantageous

The Double Consonant

Double the final single consonant when it is preceded by a vowel before adding a suffix that begins with a vowel:

bidder
trimmer
swimming
occurred

The *ie* Combination

Type *i* before *e* except after *c* or when the *ie* combination sounds like an *a*, as in *neighbor* and *weigh*.

Examples: lien
             lieu
             view
             achieve
             field

EXCEPTIONS:

Examples: receive
             deceive
             perceive
             conceit

EXCEPTIONS:

beige
sleigh
reign
their

Plurals

Most plurals are formed by adding *s* to the noun:

files	miles
checks	clubs
offices	vitamins
benefits	vacations
debts	errors
contracts	

Some plurals of words are formed by adding *es* (words that end in *ch, x, s, z,* or *sh*).

businesses	washes
boxes	buzzes
churches	mixes

The *y* Ending

To form the plural of words ending in *y* preceded by a consonant, change the *y* to *i* and add *es:*

inquiries	counties
auxiliaries	duties

To form the plural of words ending in *y* preceded by a vowel, retain the *y* and add *s:*

keys	days
rays	buys

The *f* or *fe* Ending

Some words ending in *f* or *fe* take the plural form by changing the *f* to *v* and adding *es:*

leaf becomes leaves
beef becomes beeves or beefs
hoof becomes hooves or hoofs
scarf becomes scarves or scarfs

The *o* Ending

Words ending in *o* become plural when *s* or *es* is added:
Vowel precedes *o:*

patios
cameos
studios

Consonant precedes *o*:

pianos
mottoes or mottos
dittos
zeros or zeroes
tomatoes
potatoes
heroes

Compound Words

Form the plural of compound words by adding *s* or *es* to the most important one:

    chambers of commerce
    runners-up
    mothers-in-law
    letters of credit
    certificates of deposit

Letters and Numbers

Add only *s* or *es* if the subject does not include periods:

    sixes
    FHAs
    '40s

Add *'s* to abbreviations with periods and to letters that could be misread as a word instead of the plural form:

    D.D.S.'s   i's
    Ed.D.'s   u's

WORD DIVISION

Never divide an abbreviation, contraction, or a word with a one-syllable pronunciation:

    LL.D.
    can't
    cleaned

Divide *between* syllables:

    market-able
    vegeta-tion
    resist-ance

Do not break a word if only one letter would stand alone:

    a-ward   e-vict

If at least two letters cannot be left standing at the end of the first line, carry the entire word to the second line:

    en-croach
    in-sist
    de-preciate

Compound words are to be divided where they join:

    schoolboy   school-boy
    fireplace   fire-place
    switchboard   switch-board
    keypunch   key-punch

Hyphenated words are to be divided at the end of the writing line following the hyphen:

    light-hearted fantasy   light-
    well-known firm   well-
    long-range goal   long-

Words containing two consecutive vowels should be divided between the vowels:

    vi-olation
    immedi-ately
    bi-ennial
    re-arranged

Words containing double prefixes should be divided at the end of the second prefix:

    misin-form
    unin-tentional
    inad-vertently

If it is necessary to divide numbers, place the hyphen after a comma:

    8,346,-809

Gender titles should not be separated from a proper name:

Mrs. Alan K. Warm
not: Mrs.
Alan K. Warm

Avoid dividing:

1. The last word of a paragraph
2. The last word on a page
3. More than two consecutive line-ending words
4. Capitalized words

Words containing only four letters should not be divided:

only
okay
airy

If it is necessary to separate a date, divide between the day and the year, not between the month and the day:

January 1,
19__

CAPITALIZATION

Capitalize proper nouns—all given and surnames of people and officially named places and things:

Person: Allen B. Johnson
Place: Denver, Colorado
Thing: Grayson Park

Capitalize names of government units:

Social Security Administration
Post Office Department
Federal Communications Commission

Capitalize words that are used as substitutes for a particular person, place, or thing:

Miss America
Cornhusker State
Boss of the Year Award

Capitalize the first word of each line of poetry:

> Winds of strength disturb the trees;
> Branches sway and lose their leaves.

Capitalize the first word of a direct quotation:

The visitor asked, "Where is the nearest service station?"

Capitalize the first word of each line of a menu:

> LUNCHEON
> Tomato soup   Bread sticks
> Spinach-egg salad
> Grilled cheese sandwich
> Coffee or tea

Capitalize the first word in a sentence:

The new tennis court will be finished in two months.

Capitalize titles when they are followed by a person's name:

Director Kingman
Countess Carol
Professor Evans

Capitalize holidays, historic events, days of the week, and months:

Christmas
New Year's Day
World War II
Louisiana Purchase
Monday, Tuesday, Wednesday
January, February, March, April

Capitalize special events:

Douglas County Fair
Evansville Centennial Days

Capitalize specific geographic locations:

> They are scheduled to leave for the Orient next week.
> Some of the offices on the West Coast are open all day Saturdays.
> We are now driving north on South Carver Street.

Capitalize books of the Bible and other sacred books, but do not underline them.

Capitalize words derived from proper names:

> Sanforized cloth
> Windsor tie
> Edwardian design
> English walnut
> Danish pastry

Do not capitalize words derived from proper nouns that have become common words:

> vulcanized tire
> pasteurized milk
> mercerized thread
> klieg light

TITLES

Capitalize and underline titles of *published* material: books, newspapers, magazines, reports, plays, pamphlets; movies; also titles of paintings, sculpture, lengthy poems, and operas.

Capitalize and enclose in quotation marks unpublished material, parts of published material, and short poems; also songs and other short musical works; television and radio productions.

A Manual of Style (University of Chicago Press) states rules for capitalization and punctuation of titles.

NUMBERS

Write Out:

1. Numbers that begin a sentence:

Ninety-nine members have paid their dues for this year.

2. Numbers less than one hundred:

There are fifty-three volunteers.

3. Even amounts over one hundred:

Invitations were mailed to six hundred people.

4. Expressions of time when *o'clock* is used:

Plan to leave town no later than eleven o'clock.

5. *Per cent* when used with an indefinite amount:

We estimate that six per cent of the eighty people scheduled to take the test Saturday will rate above average.

6. Days of the month when they precede the name of the month:

On this twenty-first day of January, 19--.

Consistency:

If several numbers in a sentence pertain to the same group and some of the numbers are less than one hundred but at least one number is more than one hundred, all of them may be expressed in figures:

Of the 123 enrolled in the class, 28 are short, 22 are tall, and 73 are average height.

Figures:

1. Percentages expressed in definite terms are typed in figures:

The interest rate on your loan is 6%.

2. Large amounts—millions and billions:

That field produced 6.8 million barrels of oil.
Expansion and improvements will cost $2.25 million.

3. Time expressed in hours and minutes:

The plane left at 11:45 a.m.; it arrives in New York at 6:00 p.m.

4. Time followed with abbreviations (a.m. or p.m.):

She left New York at 3 p.m. Wednesday and arrived in Europe at 8 a.m. Thursday.

5. Fractions are usually expressed in figures:

The office is 10 3/4 by 11 1/2 feet.

6. References to printed material:

Read page 83.

7. Days when they follow the name of the month:

January 6, 19--

8. Stock quotations:

They bought at 10 1/4 and sold at 20 1/2.

9. Telephone numbers:

(101) 492-3886

10. File references:

Policy No. 113829
Order No. 6314
File G-1090

11. Age stated in detail:

He is 21 years, 3 months, 4 days old.

12. Game scores:

St. Louis   16
Boston   10

13. Building numbers in addresses:

301 East 59th Avenue

14. Suite numbers in addresses:

42 North 51st Street, Suite 314

Money:

Even sums of money may be written as figures.

Submit the bill for approval after you add $19 to the total.

Cents without dollars may be written as figures.

Her favorite pen cost 98 cents.

Consecutive Numbers:

Type one of the amounts in figures:

She read four 325-word pages in two minutes.
The farmer bought two 4-row planters.

ABBREVIATIONS

Whenever space is available, write out the words except where abbreviations are *always* used: Mr., Mrs., Dr.; and Jr. and Sr. following surnames; also academic degrees that follow a surname (M.D., Ph.D., Ed.D., D.D.S., etc.).

Do not abbreviate firm names unless papers that come into your office from the respective firms show such names abbreviated, then follow the same style of writing that appears on the incoming papers.

If, for example, a letterhead imprint reads "Mills & Patton," address outgoing correspondence the same as the letterhead imprint.

It may be necessary to abbreviate because of limited space on office forms, but the abbreviation must be one that will not be confusing to anyone unfamiliar with the work.

Never abbreviate *and* in the heading of a letter:

TYPE: Mr. and Mrs. Andrew Oaks
NEVER: Mr. & Mrs. Andrew Oaks

Ordinals are not followed by a period: 1st, 2nd, 3rd, 4th.

Familiar abbreviations are formed with capital letters and no periods:

FBI   IRS   FHA   MST   POD   GOP

United States may be abbreviated when it precedes a noun, but it must be spelled out when it follows a noun:

U.S. Supreme Court
Supreme Court of the United States

If *full names* follow the titles *Reverend* and *Honorable*, the titles may be abbreviated (Rev., Hon.). Reverend is spelled out when preceded by *the;* for example, the Reverend Dr. Sands or the Reverend Harvey S. Sands.

10

Make the Typewriter Work for You

The key to typing any assignment is to become the master of the typewriter by making it work for *you*.

Knowing how to set your typewriter for various tasks should take the toughness out of typing assignments.

Keep the typewriter in good working condition and learn how to operate your particular machine. Manuals usually come with the typewriter at the time it is purchased. These manuals should remain with their typewriters. The manuals are not to be allowed to become mutilated and tossed in a bottom drawer, eventually to disappear from the office.

When a typewriter is replaced by a different machine, return the corresponding manual with the typewriter so that the new owner of your "old" machine will be able to refer to the manual for operating suggestions.

Learn how to change the typewriter ribbon. Read the manual that accompanies the typewriter and follow the instructions for replacing the ribbon when necessary.

Perhaps you can help cut office expenses by not having your typewriter serviced merely for the purpose of replacing the ribbon. Consider, also, the wasted time when each time the ribbon is replaced your typewriter is idle and so are you. Find out exactly which lever affects the ribbon reverse, then insert the ribbon correctly.

The typewriter should rest on a sturdy base. Support is important; it should not be necessary for you to interrupt your concentration and typing intermittently to retrieve your typewriter.

Care of the Typewriter.   At the end of each working day, brush the erasure crumbs from the typewriter onto the table or stand; from the table, brush them into the wastepaper basket. Wipe carbon smudges from the surface of the machine. Cover the typewriter every night. If the machine is electric, turn it off when it is not in use during the workday as well as at the end of the day.

Keep the type bars clean. There should be no filled letters; they should all be clear of residue for sharp impressions. Type-cleaning products are available at office-supply stores, so caring for your typewriter need not be a chore.

Erasing at the Typewriter.   Move the carriage (release the margin stop) as far as possible to the side on which the error appears. Brush, don't blow, the erasure crumbs away from the type bars.

If the error is on the left side of the center of the paper, move the carriage as far to the left as possible; if the error is on the right side of the center of the paper, move the carriage to the right as far as possible—release the margin stops. The margin must again be reset; but if the typewriter is in the best working condition, this should be simple. If the margin stops do not reset in the proper place, the typewriter apparently needs some adjustment. (The appearance of typed material depends on the upkeep of the typist's tool as well as the ability to type.)

Some secretaries prefer eraser guards or shields for erasing; others prefer slips of paper, to eliminate the carbon smudge that the edge of a heavy erasing tool leaves on the copy from pressure applied while erasing.

If slips of paper are used, always insert the slips behind the carbon paper, and allow approximately one-half inch to protrude from the side of the papers being erased; otherwise, the slips can easily be left in the machine—the typing shows up on the slip of paper and not on the copies.

Number the slips to be inserted when making erasures in both corners at the top of the slip (Figure 10-1). If the slips of paper are numbered in both corners, the numbers will show when the slips protrude from the left side of the carbon pack; and the numbers will also show when an erasure is made on the right side of the carbon pack (Figure 10-2). After making the erasure, pull the slips

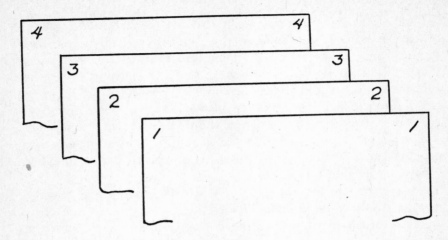

Figure 10-1. Numbered Slips of Paper Used When Erasing at the Typewriter.

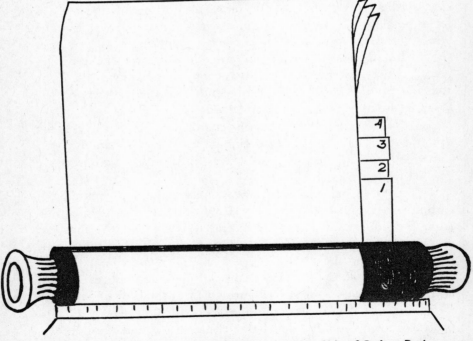

Figure 10-2. Numbered Slips of Paper Protrude from Side of Carbon Pack on Which Error Appears.

out of the machine and immediately check the numbers to make sure no slip has remained within the carbon pack.

Of course, the slips of paper would not be as durable as an eraser guard.

Sometimes the backing on carbon paper discolors the reverse side of the typing paper, particularly when slips of paper are used during the erasing process instead of an eraser guard. Check the reverse side of the paper; and if, by erasing, some of the color has been transferred to the typing paper, erase this smudge when you remove the paper from the typewriter.

Erasing at the Bottom of the Page.   Turn the cylinder knob backward until the error at the bottom of the page can be placed on the platen, then erase. If you turn the cylinder forward for "erasing room," the paper can inadvertently be eased up and out of alignment.

Realigning the Paper.   When you must reinsert paper on which typed material appears, position the paper so that the type bar strikes in the exact position as the typed line. Switch the ribbon control lever to stencil and strike one letter for correct alignment. If the letter is properly aligned, return the ribbon control lever to its original position and type the letter or word. (One exception to this is in Chapter 12, where the paper is inserted for one-word corrections and no additional typing will be affected by the alignment explained for correcting errors.)

Punctuating at the Typewriter.

Do not space—

    before or after a hyphen
    before or after a dash

Space once after a—

    comma
    semicolon
    period when used with initials (L.C. King; A.B. Nob)

Space twice after a—

    period indicating end of sentence
    colon

Race-with-Time Chores.   Before you begin typing the race-with-time chores, set the margin stops, the line spacer, the tabulator, and whatever other lever you will be using during the assignment of mass production—cards, envelopes, or statements.

Card Stacks.   The first card typed must be inserted from behind the cylinder. Type the card. Before you remove the card, insert the second card in front of the cylinder but behind the card which you just finished typing. The first card should pull the second card into typing position as you turn the cylinder backward. Using this system, the cards will stack up against the paper rest with the typed material away from you. If the cards are typed in alphabetical order, this will present no problem because the cards will remain in order if you place each stack face down on the preceding stack. Three or four spaces extending from the front of the cylinder should be sufficient to pull the new insertion into the typewriter and around the cylinder. It may be necessary to adjust some of the cards so that the typing line will be straight.

Typing Envelopes.   When all other speed systems for typing envelopes fail, maybe this one will be worth trying. Place the envelopes face down, flap side up (Figure 10-3).

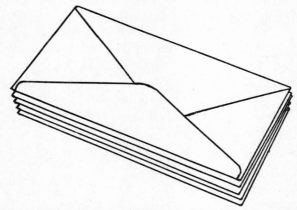

Figure 10-3. Envelope Stack Placement for Production Typing.

With your right hand, pick up the envelope deep into the flap fold so that the thumb and second finger are opposite one another. Place the flap end deep into the typewriter behind the cylinder. At the same time, with your left hand, turn the cylinder knob forward to expose the envelope for typing position. Type. With the left hand on the cylinder knob and the right hand at the top of the typed envelope, turn the cylinder knob forward and pull the envelope out of the typewriter with the right hand. With the left hand still on the cylinder knob, push the carriage to the right—into beginning typing position. Place the typed envelope (which you hold in your right hand) face down and pick up the second envelope. Insert the second envelope, using the same procedure as above. When you remove the second envelope and all other envelopes, place them face down and behind the flap of each preceding envelope. This will keep the flaps free and up, ready for machine or hand sealing. It also eliminates having to go through the entire stack later to pull out the flaps.

The hand movements are quick. Little time is spent releasing the paper release lever, in order to position the envelope for a straight typing line, when the single envelope insertion method is used. The paper release lever would be in "closed" position when the envelopes are inserted.

Drafting Material.   When you type a rough draft, indicate at the top of the paper that it is a "Draft." Set the margins the same as for the final copy, but double space the draft. Final copy margin stops should allow sufficient space for handwritten notations. These margins along with double spacing should enable the person for whom the draft is being typed to make necessary corrections or insertions. Spelling, punctuation, capitalization, and paragraphing should be correct.

Perhaps the only difference between draft presentation and final copy, other than the line spacing, will be the revision and additions made by the individual who assigned the work to you.

Words and Figures on Lined Paper.   Ruled paper packs that are pre-assembled and bound at the time of purchase usually do not create the problem that besets the typist who must align several sheets which have been reproduced within the office.

Keep a stapler handy. Hold the sheets of paper up to the light or window, and match the lines. Insert the stapled sheets into the typewriter just enough to hold them around the cylinder, then insert the carbon paper between these sheets and roll the entire pack into the machine. Staples may then be removed after the packet is in the typewriter, if you must erase.

Do not type on the line. Type approximately 1/16 of an inch above the line, if you must make carbon copies on ruled lines. Sometimes the typed letters on carbon copies "spread." If you allow for this letter "spread" by typing above the ruled lines, the carbon copies will be easy to read and the letters will clear the ruled line.

The Tabulator.   Use the tabulator for speed. Again, the typewriter must be in good working condition. When the tab set does not hold, or if it does not clear properly, a typing assignment can become anything but neat and attractive.

In an office where you use the same letterhead and the same letter style, set the tabulator for the date, paragraph indentations, subject line, complimentary close, and signature line.

Use the tabulator when you type columns of figures and lists. Set tabs when statements are typed, or when any mass production typing job is assigned to you and the information must appear in a specific place.

Set tabs for indenting paragraphs. Always indent paragraphs when double spacing or triple spacing material.

Before you set the tabulator for any typing assignment, clear the typewriter of all other tabs. Set the tab stops for the project at hand. Check the stops before you begin typing.

Centering a Typing Project.   A sheet of paper measuring 8 ½ by 11 inches has *85* horizontal spaces of *pica* type; there is a count of *102* horizontal spaces of *elite* type. The vertical space count is 66 for both pica and elite type.

For elite type, the centering figure is 51; the pica centering point is 42, when typing on 8½ by 11 inch paper. Vertically the centering point is 33 for both sizes of type. See Figures 10-4 and 10-5.

To center material on a page horizontally you must subtract the total number of letters, numbers, and separating spaces needed within the assignment from the total number of spaces available on the size of paper being used.

To center material vertically, subtract the number of type-lines and separating lines needed for the project from the available vertical spaces, and divide by one half.

Here is an example for centering a title, using pica type and an 8½ by 11 inch page: Forty-two is the centering figure (Figure 10-4). One half of the title must appear to the left of 42, and one half of the title must appear to the right of 42. Starting at 42 on the carriage scale, backspace once for every two letters and

CENTERING

PICA TYPE: 85 spaces on paper measuring 8 1/2 inches wide.
The center of the paper when no allowance is made for binding
is 42.

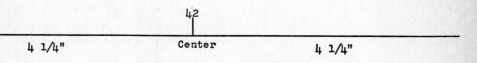

The center of the paper when one inch is allowed for binding
is 47.

Ten spaces measure one inch.

Calculation: Add one half of the one inch allowed for binding,
              or five spaces (10 spaces divided by 2 = 5), to
              the original center of 42 for the new center of
              47.

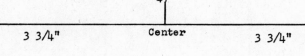

Figure 10-4. Centering Calculation and Measurement for Pica Type.

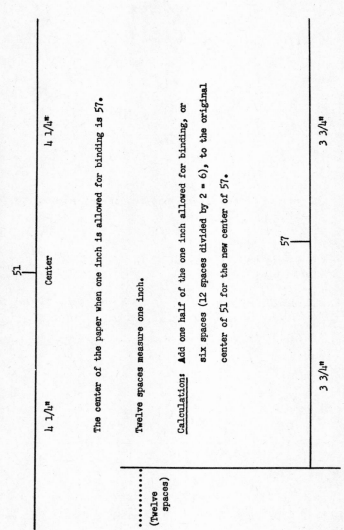

CENTERING

ELITE TYPE: 102 spaces on paper measuring 8 1/2 inches wide. The center of the paper when no allowance is made for binding is 51.

4 1/4"   Center   4 1/4"

51

The center of the paper when one inch is allowed for binding is 57.

Twelve spaces measure one inch.

Calculation: Add one half of the one inch allowed for binding, or six spaces (12 spaces divided by 2 = 6), to the original center of 51 for the new center of 57.

(Twelve spaces)

3 3/4"   57   3 3/4"

Figure 10-5. Centering Calculation and Measurement for Elite Type.

separating spaces within the title. The title is: "How to Center a Title." There are twenty-one letters and separating spaces in the title; ten letters and separating spaces will appear to the left of 42 and eleven letters and separating spaces will appear to the right of 42. Begin typing the title at 32 on the carriage scale.

42

HOW TO CENTER A TITLE

Centering can also be figured mathematically. Count the letters and separating spaces in the title; divide the total, 21, by one half—disregard the remaining space. Ten spaces subtracted from the centering figure, 42, puts the first stroke of the title at 32 on the carriage scale.

If your typewriter has a wide carriage and there are 130 spaces on the scale but the paper measures ten inches wide, you have only the width of the paper with which to work. In this case, you would have 120 spaces for figuring. You could set the margins first and center the material between these selected margins. The centering figure for ten-inch wide paper, using elite type, is 60; and the material to be centered by backspacing would begin at 60 on the carriage scale.

Centering for Binding.   When material must be bound either at the top or at the side, allowance must be made for margins before the material to be typed is figured from the centering point because the centering figure changes (Figure 10-5).

For side-bound papers, allowing one-half inch for binding, the center is *51 plus three spaces* (one-half inch equals six elite spaces) *or 54.*

If you have a two-inch left margin and *one inch* is needed for binding, the centering point (for elite type) would be 51 plus one half of the extra one-inch left margin, or 57. (Twelve spaces of elite-size type equal one inch; divide twelve spaces by one half, which equals six spaces. Add six spaces to the centering figure of 51 for this particular example of allowance for binding at the side.)

Horizontal Spacing of Tables. After the title is centered, use the longest line as your guide for centering the information horizontally. To do this, count the number of letters, numbers, and spaces needed. Subtract this count from the total number of spaces available on the paper.

Tables may be single or double spaced, depending on the length of the table and on office specifications.

SCHOOL SUPPLIES

(1)	(2)	(3)
Elementary	*Secondary*	*High School*
Crayons	Art supplies	Binders
Construction paper	Compasses	Brushes
Dictionary	Dictionary	Charts
Pencils	Notebooks	Graph paper
Workbooks	Pencils	Lab equipment

Figure 10-6. Centered Horizontally (Pica Type).

Heading. If the heading for table columns does not exceed the number of spaces needed for the items to be listed, the table may be set up with all columnar headings beginning at the left edge of the listing.

In Column 1, "Construction paper" is longer than the heading, "Elementary"; in Column 2, "Art supplies" is longer than "Secondary"; in Column 3, "Lab equipment" is longer than "High School."

Spacing. Triple space between title and the columnar headings; double space between columnar headings and the items listed.

Computation for "School Supplies" Table. To figure the tab stops for the three columns, using pica type, 8½ by 11 inch paper, 1½ inch left margin and one inch right margin, compute the number of spaces remaining—ten horizontal spaces to an inch of pica-size type.

The margins will take 25 spaces out of the total horizontal space count of 85, leaving 60 spaces for the three columns.

Count the letters and separating spaces in the longest item in each column. Column 1 will take 18 spaces; Column 2 will take 12 spaces; and Column 3 will take 13 spaces. Total spaces needed for the three columns is 43.

Subtract the total spaces needed from available spaces, 60 less 43 equals 17. The 17 spaces will be divided between the two dividers that form three columns. Leave eight spaces between Column 1 and Column 2; leave nine spaces between Column 2 and Column 3.

Set the tab stops. The left margin is the beginning of the first column—15 on the carriage scale:

15
Elementary

Figure the second column tab stop. Count the spaces needed for the longest line in the first column:

Construction paper =	18 spaces
Plus:	
Spaces between first	
and second columns	8 spaces
Add	26
to first tab stop	15
Second tab stop is:	41

15   41
Elementary   *Secondary*

Figure the third column tab stop. Count the spaces needed for the longest line in the second column:

Art supplies =	12 spaces
Plus:	
Spaces between sec-	
ond and third	
columns	9 spaces
Add	21
to second tab stop	41
Third tab stop is:	62

15   41   62
Elementary   *Secondary*   *High School*

Sixty-two, the third tab stop, plus the thirteen spaces needed for "Lab equipment" equals 75; ten spaces—one inch of pica type—remain to become the right margin.

The next illustration Figure 10-7 is a horizontally centered table using elite type. Computations for "Inventory List" follow.

INVENTORY LIST

Washable Fabrics

Bolts	Printed	Plain	Striped	Checked
Cotton	12	10	12	10
Wool	25	15	14	8
Nylon	9	25	16	6
Totals	46	50	42	24

Figure 10-7. Centered Horizontally (Elite Type).

Computation for Table and Elite Type.   Figure 10-7, "Inventory List," is arranged on a sheet of paper 8½ by 11 inches with a two and one-half inch left margin and a two-inch right margin. Elite type has twelve spaces to the horizontal inch. The margins take up 54 of the total 102 spaces, leaving 48 spaces for the contents of the table. A total of fourteen spaces are needed for typing, leaving 34 spaces to be divided among the five columns or four divider areas. The four dividing areas into 34 spaces allows eight spaces between columns with two spaces remaining. The two remaining spaces may be added to the right margin.

The first column is typed at 30 (the end of the two and one-half inch left margin) on the carriage scale.

(30)
Bolts

Six spaces are needed for the longest word in the first column plus eight divider spaces. Add these two numbers (six and eight are fourteen) to 30 for the figure at which to begin the second column—the tab stop is 44.

(30)   (44)
Bolts   *Printed*

Two spaces plus eight divider spaces added to 44 is the beginning of the third column—54.

(30)	(44)	(54)
Bolts		
Cotton	12	10

The beginning of the fourth column is ten spaces added to 54, or 64.

(30)	(44)	(54)	(64)
Bolts			
Cotton	12	10	12

The beginning of the fifth column is ten spaces added to 64, or 74.

(30)	(44)	(54)	(64)	(74)
Bolts				
Cotton	12	10	12	10

Spaces 74 and 75 are used for typing the fifth column, leaving twenty-six spaces (two inches plus two extra spaces) for the right margin.

Heading. All headings in a table must be centered over the longest line in the respective columns *when any heading within* the table is longer than the items listed beneath it.

To center the columnar headings, count the number of spaces needed for the longest item listed and count the spaces needed for the heading. Subtract and divide the answer by two. Backspace or tap the space bar the number of times needed to center the heading over the column. Example: There are "12" bolts of "Printed" cotton. Two spaces are needed to type "12." Seven spaces are needed for "Printed." The difference is five, and five divided by two is: two and three. Backspace from the tab stop twice to center the word "Printed" over its column.

Vertical Spacing. A sheet of paper eleven inches long has 66 vertical spaces, using either size type, pica or elite.

To center material vertically, count the type-lines needed plus the spaces separating the type-lines from columnar headings, table title, and the subtitle.

STATE FAIR WINNERS

Domestic Arts

Class	Winner
Baking	Alice Finch
Canning	Betty Gayer
Cooking	Cora Hill
Freezing	Dorothy Inns
Sewing	Ellen Jewel

Figure 10-8. Centered Vertically.

Figure 10-8, "State Fair Winners," is centered vertically. This is the procedure:

Type-lines needed: 8
Separating lines needed: 8
Total lines needed: 16
Subtract 16 from 66 for a balance of 50 lines.
Divide 50 by one half (50 ÷ ½ = 25)
Type the title 25 spaces from the top of the page.

Title and Subtitle Spacing.   Space twice between title and subtitle. Space three times between subtitle and columnar headings; space twice between columnar headings and the list. Underline the columnar headings.

"Spread" Typing.   To center a "spread" title or heading, space once for each letter-space count. Consider the letters and all separating spaces in the title as you backspace from center. For the count, space once between letters making up the words, and space three times between each word. Or, count all separating spaces and letters and divide by one half to find the starting point from the left side of the page (Figure 10-9).

Periods as "Leaders."   When you type these eye-guiding periods, leave one space following the last word and one space before the dollar sign, as shown in Figure 10-10. When numbers

CLASSES VIEWING FILMS

Fall Semester

MORNING SESSIONS

Class	Attendance
History	98
Biology	102
Zoology	75
English	125
Art	50
Drama	45

AFTERNOON SESSIONS

Class	Attendance
Music	60
Political Science	45
Economics	35
Psychology	90

Figure 10-9. Spread Typing.

STATEMENT OF REVENUE

June 1, 19-- to May 31, 19--

Airport Fund	$ 5,076.31
Bond Levy Fund	60,225.99
General Fund	90,625.55
Light Fund	20,111.62
Park Fund	16,347.77
Sewer Fund	38,100.61
Water Fund	61,080.02
Total	$291,567.87

Figure 10-10. Leaders.

are not expressed as dollar amounts, use the largest number as the guide for striking the last period.

Leaders must be aligned and generally they are spread across the page by alternately striking the period and the space bar. Make a mental or handwritten note as soon as you strike the first period that begins the guide line: "The period begins on an even (or uneven) number on the carriage scale."

The Dollar Sign.   Dollar signs in a table must be aligned. The dollar sign appears on the first line of the table and also with the total amount. It is not typed on every line within the table.

Allow for this character when you space a table. Check the total amount before you type the dollar sign on the first line of the table. It may be necessary to leave nore than one space between the dollar sign and the amount opposite it.

The Tabulator and Dollar Amounts.   Allow space for the dollar sign, but set the tabulator stop when typing columns of figures at the point where the majority of the listings begin. Backspace for the larger figures and use the space bar to align smaller figures. For example, turn to Figure 10-11, "Mid-Year Report." Set the tab at the point where you would begin typing the hundred thousand dollar amounts; there are seven listings in the two columns. Only one figure in both columns makes it necessary to indent; and the two total figures make it necessary to

Datime Corporation

MID-YEAR REPORT

June 30, 19--

Item	Predicted Sales	Actual Sales
Chairs	$ 401,000	$ 400,000
Desks	400,000	415,000
Filing cabinets	89,421	120,000
Typewriters	590,000	652,391
TOTALS	$1,480,421	$1,587,391

Figure 10-11. Tab Stops: Hundred Thousand Figure.

backspace. Indenting and backspacing for only three column listings take less time than indenting each of the figures in the two columns if the tabulator stop is set for the dollar sign.

Financial Reports. Often, financial reports are prepared by a printer; figures are the only insertions required to complete the report for company records.

Sometimes the dollar sign is also printed on the form; and as few as two tab stops are set by the typist. Check the total amount before you begin typing, to determine how many spaces must be allowed between the dollar sign and the amounts smaller than the total. All dollars and cents will then be in proper alignment.

Figure 10-12, "Statement of Assets and Liabilities," in more detail, possibly would be presented to you as a printed form. Only the figures would be typed in the blanks.

Datime Corporation

STATEMENT OF ASSETS AND LIABILITIES

December 31, 19--

ASSETS

Cash on deposit		$ 20,891.43
U. S. Government Securities		96,019.69
Receivables:		
Dividends	$52,000.25	
Interest	12,891.16	
Furniture and Equipment		64,891.41
Investments		17,256.84
		108,425.00
TOTAL ASSETS		$307,484.37

LIABILITIES

Accounts Payable	$ 70,500.00
Miscellaneous Accrued Expenses	21,296.05
Bonds Payable	115,688.32
Capital	60,000.00
Surplus	40,000.00
TOTAL LIABILITIES AND CAPITAL	$307,484.37

Figure 10-12. Financial Report.

There may be any number of reports to be typed in an office. If a copy of a financial report is available, follow the arrangement as previously typed, unless it is so obvious that the arrangement is not the best one. Your "better" arrangement must meet your supervisor's approval before you present a finished copy to him.

Usually a copy of the report is set aside as a working copy;

Down 16 spaces   (45)
              Datime Corporation
       (42)
        OPERATING EXPENSE REPORT*

June 30, 19--

	(57) Departments		
(33) Item	(52) Office	(65) Sales	(75) Laboratory
(24) Equipment and Machinery	$ 3,463	$ ---	$ 25,687
Furniture and Fixtures	8,600	1,026	200
Insurance and Taxes	5,225	8,424	10,989
Maintenance	2,600	4,500	8,000
Raw Material	---	10,375	26,952
Rent	500	600	700
Salaries	38,800	50,000	74,000
Supplies	1,241	425	600
Utilities	225	100	873
TOTALS	$60,654	$75,450	$148,001

*Amounts figured to nearest dollar.

Figure 10-13. "Working Copy."

changes for the new report appear opposite the last report figures either in pen or pencil, and the old figures are blotted out, lines drawn through them, or an "X" is marked through them.

The report may also have staples or fasteners intact; but because it is a working copy, staples and fasteners can be removed and the sheets used as guides for tab stops. Set the margin stops and tab stops from these working sheets—no need to figure spacing. Vertical spacing can also be handled in the same manner.

The same reports with the same headings will probably be typed for the same meetings month after month, and year after year, only the amounts change perhaps. Reports can be typed quickly if the typist uses the previous sheet as a guide for setting tab stops and margins.

If no working copy is available, make an extra copy of the first report you type. Pencil or type in red, in parentheses, on your reference copy the tab stops above each title, heading, and figure column. Dates change, so this will be centered each time the date is typed.

Figure 10-13, "Operating Expense Report," shows the vertical spacing and tab stops as they would appear on a working copy. This is to eliminate re-figuring the tab stops each time the report is typed.

Some firms show two or three related reports on one sheet instead of typing very short reports on separate sheets.

Vertical spacing for multiple reports on one sheet would be determined by the number of spaces remaining after allowance has been made for the number of lines needed for each report, plus the separating spaces to distinguish one report from another.

11

Special Typing Projects

Classified as special typing projects, in this chapter, are business
reports and the preliminary pages, recording the minutes of
meetings, and preparing press releases.

REPORTS IN BUSINESS

Reports of several pages that present the business activity in
writing usually are preceded by a title page or cover sheet, and a
table of contents. Every report, condensed or lengthy, should be
identified.

Cover Page.   Two items plus the company emblem or other
appropriate design may appear on this page: (1) the title of the
report, and (2) the name of the person who compiled the
information for the report.

Title Page.   These items appear on the title page: (1) the
title of the report; (2) the name of the person who compiled the
report or the name of the department or district, submitted
through the individual in charge of the business area; and (3) the
date.

The title page, or cover page, is page one but the numeral is not
typed on the page (Figure 11-1).

Table of Contents.   The table of contents follows the title
page and would be page two of the report. This second page is
visibly marked with small Roman numerals, and it is the *first page
to show a page number.* The title page or cover page would be
page one, understood, but not visible.

MID-YEAR SALES ANALYSIS

of

D A T I M E   C O R P O R A T I O N

Denver, Colorado

Submitted to

S. T. WILLIAMS
Vice President/Sales

By

U. V. Taler
District Sales Manager

Casper, Wyoming

JUNE 30, 19--

Figure 11-1. Title Page.

The table of contents (Figure 11-2) is typed after the final copy of the report is typed. Page numbers are to be typed one directly beneath the other. Periods, as an eye-guide, are also to be vertically aligned.

Margins for Reports.   The first line on the first page of the report and the first page of following chapters begin on the

C O N T E N T S

Page

Figure 11-2. Table of Contents.

thirteenth line from the top of the page. This leaves a two-inch margin for these opening pages.

All other pages have a one-inch top margin:

1. If the report is bound at the side, the page number begins on the seventh line; and the first line of typed material begins on the tenth line.

2. If the report is bound at the top, the typing begins on line ten. This allows one-half inch for binding and one inch as the visible margin. The right margin and the bottom margins should be no less than one inch.

Spacing for Reports.   Allow for margins and page number placement. Double space the discourse part of the report, unless you are instructed to single space. If your typewriter can be set for one and one-half spaces, this spacing may be adequate for the report.

Page Numbers.   Identify introductory pages by small Roman numerals. Number the "report" pages with Arabic numerals.

If you bind the report at the top, type the page numbers one-half inch from the bottom of the page (three spaces), in the center of the paper. Page numbers placed in this position may be framed with hyphens (-5-).

Type the page number on line seven, flush with the right margin if the report is to be fastened on the left. Double space; begin the first line of type on the tenth line.

When you number pages at the top, do not frame the number with hyphens, just type the number.

Headings for the Report.   Reports are important. They should be typed accurately, neatly, and the important introductory words should be stressed with the typewriter. Capital letters and the underlining system, many times, are sufficient to signify importance and to draw attention to these words (Figure 11-3).

Type the *main heading* in the center of the page in capital letters.

Type the *subheading* either in the center of the page or flush with the left margin, but be consistent throughout the report. The subheadings may be typed in capital letters or underlined with only the first letter of the important words capitalized.

Indented headings form the first part of a paragraph; they are underlined.

Numbered Sentences.   Both styles that follow are acceptable; but use one style consistently throughout the typing assignment.

Pattern No. 1:
1.   Indent the number and begin typing two spaces following the period. Carry-over lines begin directly beneath the first letter of the preceding sentence line.
2.   Follow the same pattern for all succeeding items that are to be listed.

Pattern No. 2:
   1. Indent the number, followed by a period. Begin typing two spaces after the period and start the carry-over lines at the left margin.
   2. Follow the same pattern for all succeeding items that are to be listed.

Quoted Material.   Brief quotations may be enclosed in

H E A D I N G S

This is a main heading: COMPETITIVE SALES

                                           Several factors were considered when

                                           statistics were compiled to represent the

                                           volume and dollar totals.

                                           The totals were compared with figures

                                           of other firms that deal in the same product.

This is a subheading: QUALITY

    (It can cover more   Our product is rated "top quality." It

than one paragraph.)   is more durable than similarly manufactured

                                products sold in this area.

                                           The finished product is a combination of

                                raw material, equipment, and technique.

These are indented

    headings: Components used in the manufacturing

    (They identify separate   process are of the best grade.

paragraphs.)   Experience is also in our favor--surveys

                                reveal that our trained-employee average is

                                two years.

Figure 11-3. Report Headings.

quotation marks; longer quotations, three or more lines, should be
set in several spaces from the margins and single spaced.

> *Example:*   Neatness and accuracy are musts in the
>   office. . . . Mathematical calculations sometimes give
>   way to accurate estimates with typing experience.

Type the quotation as it appears in the text from which it was
extracted. If the quotation is the forepart of a paragraph or the
entire paragraph, show this by indenting the first line of the
quotation. If the first line of the quotation is not the beginning of
a paragraph as originally printed, do not indent the first line in
your copy.

REVIEW OF THE OUTLINE

In an office, requests for an outline may be few and far
between, but a sample is included for review (Figure 11-4).

```
                    OFFICE REMINDERS

   I.  Daily Chores

       A.  Morning duties
           1.  Switch lights on
           2.  Mark appointment calendars
               a.  Boss' office
               b.  Secretary's office
           3.  Change date stamp
           4.  Fill water Thermos
       B.  Afternoon duties
           1.  Lock desk
           2.  Lock files
           3.  Switch lights off
               a.  Boss' office
               b.  Secretary's office

  II.  Regular Meetings

       A.  Weekly
           1.  Thursday afternoon
               a.  Office Personnel
               b.  Purchasing Department
           2.  Friday morning
               a.  Public Relations Department
               b.  Service Department
       B.  Monthly
           1.  Accounting Department
           2.  Board of Directors
```

Figure 11-4. Outline.

The main headings are assigned Roman numerals. Subheadings
are assigned capital letters, and additional divisions are marked
with Arabic numerals and small letters. The foregoing numerals
and letters are followed with periods.

Further divisions are Arabic numerals and small letters enclosed
in parentheses, but they are not followed with periods.

Topics or sentences, whichever form the outline takes, must be
listed in no less than two divisions after the primary heading has

been established. If there is an "A" there must also be a "B"; if there is a "1" there must be a "2." *Divisions, classifications,* or *segments* consist of *more than one.*

The periods that follow the numerals and letters must be aligned. One-page outlines should be vertically centered; multiple page outlines should be arranged with ample top, bottom, and side margins.

Double space between the Roman numeral headings and the capital-letter division, "A"; double space before typing a division introduced by a Roman numeral. Other divisions are single spaced.

The divisions following the main headings are indented.

MINUTES OF MEETINGS

A record of proceedings enlightens committee or board members who were absent from the preceding meeting; the written record serves as a review of the meeting for those who did attend the previous meeting; and these records become a permanent compilation of business activities in time sequence.

There are board meetings, stockholders' meetings, committee meetings, annual meetings, regular meetings, and special meetings.

Bylaws may prescribe a fixed number of members must assemble before business is transacted. This assembly, referred to as "quorum," varies with corporations. At a meeting of stockholders, quorum is based upon the number of shares represented, unless there are other standards on which quorum is based. At a meeting of directors, quorum is based on individual count, disregarding share ownership, but the "individual count" may vary with each organization.

Preparations for the meetings should include the typing of resolutions to be introduced at the meetings. Resolutions previously typed on a separate sheet may then be referred to when recording the meeting on the official minute sheets.

Typing the Meeting Minutes.   Type a rough draft of the minutes for approval before you type the final copy in the minute book.

Generally the minutes include, concisely, the following:

- The group designation (committee, board, or stockholders' meeting)
- Description of the meeting (annual, regular, or special)
- Time and place of meeting (date, hour, and location)
- Presiding officer
- Attendance (list of individuals present or quorum)
- Reading of minutes of last meeting, and approval of same
- Reports and whatever other business for which the meeting was called
- Adjournment
- Signature lines.

The arrangement of the recorded minutes, just as other business practices, varies. Follow the same form within your office each time you type the minutes. The secretary who reads the minutes can then follow a definite procedure, and the agenda can be prepared in the future from this format.

If a pattern for recording the minutes has been established within the office, follow that style.

Minute sheets vary in size. Some are bound at the top, others have slots for books that lock at the side. Some corporations use pre-numbered sheets, some do not number the minute sheets. One corporation may condense the minutes to one side of a numbered page, single spaced; another may double space the minutes and use several number-free sheets.

If four sides of the minute sheets are needed, number them, omitting the typed number "1" but including the first side of the sheet in the count. Numbers visible would then be "2," "3," "4." If the sheets are bound at the top, number the sheets at the bottom; if the sheets are bound at the side, number the sheets flush with the right-hand margin.

Usually the margins and indentations are left to the discretion of the typist. One secretary neither single spaces nor double spaces; she sets the space regulator at one and a half spaces for the text, single spaces the resolutions, and double spaces between paragraphs. Paragraphs are indented ten spaces, and the attendance and absentee lists are indented an additional ten spaces.

Letter Perfect Minutes.   Unless you are instructed to type and retype the minutes of meetings until you can produce a perfect copy, find out which of the following typewriter error correction aids you may use: (1) eraser, (2) correcting fluid, (3) correcting tape. Perhaps you may use any one of the above error correction aids.

Sizeable errors—those involving an entire line or more—cannot be corrected neatly by one of the above methods. The final copy of the minutes becomes a part of the organization's permanent records; therefore, the corporation may feel that it is worth the time to retype an entire sheet before the minutes are presented to the designated officials for signature.

If the minute sheets are pre-numbered, perhaps a system could be worked out in the office so that no questions would arise if a page must be retyped. Possibly several blank sheets could be ordered along with the numbered sheets. Keep a record of the number of blank sheets ordered and used. Such a record may resemble the illustration (Figure 11-5).

MINUTE SHEET RECORD

Date	Explanation	Blank Sheet Count	Approved (Two Officers)
1-10-	Ordered 100 pre-numbered sheets (Nos. 101 through 200)		
1-10-	Ordered 25 blank sheets (See Purchase Order No. 9645)	25	
2-24-	Used one blank sheet to replace sheet numbered 102-103 (Uncorrectable error: Paragraph 5, omitted motion)	-1	*A.B. George, V.P.* *L.C. Dill, Exec. V.P.*
2-24-	Blank sheets on hand	24	

Figure 11-5. Minute Sheet Record.

Accuracy and concentration are musts; and although ordinarily you are permitted to camouflage errors, reduce your typing speed, if necessary, to avoid typographical errors (Figure 11-6).

DATIME CORPORATION

MINUTES OF BOARD OF DIRECTORS' MEETING

February 20, 19___

    The regular meeting of the Board of Directors of Datime Corporation was held at its offices at 1250 Blank Street, City, State, on Tuesday, February 20, 19___ at 3:30 p.m. in the Conference Room. The meeting was called to order by M. N. Olson, Chairman of the Board, who also presided at the meeting.

    The following directors, constituting a majority and quorum, were present:

> A. B. Owns
> Charles D. Decker
> E. Francis Wild, M.D.
> G. H. Hillman
> I. J. Kanlish

    The following director was absent:

> K. L. Tart

    Also present was Secretary of the Board, P. Q. Roth, who acted as Secretary for the meeting.

    The secretary stated that notice of the meeting had been given to each of the directors by telephone on Wednesday, February 14, 19___. It was moved by Director Owns, seconded by Director Decker, and unanimously carried, to accept this as an official notice of the meeting.

    The secretary announced that the minutes of the special Board Meeting held on February 2, 19___ were mailed to individual members of the Board. On motion duly made, seconded, and unanimously carried, these minutes were approved.

    The chairman read the report from the Personnel Department which stated that six new employees had been hired to fill two vacancies, created

Figure 11-6. Minutes of Board of Directors' Meetings.

157

by individuals returning to college, and to adequately fill the need for

additional help in the expanded Real Estate Department. On motion duly

made, seconded, and unanimously carried, the report was accepted and

ordered filed.

        Earnings for the past month were reported by the chairman to

be 3½% above those reported a month ago. Expenses also increased by

1½% in the last month.

        On motion duly made, seconded, and unanimously carried, the

following resolution, introduced by Director Hillman, was approved:

        "Whereas, Salaries paid are to be in line with the
cost of living; the members of the Board have been presented
facts and figures for consideration and review; and it is
considered that the best interest of said Corporation will be
subserved by complying with cost of living requirements; be it

        Resolved, That all salaries paid to employees will
begin at no less than _____ Dollars ($_____) per hourly
wage, and no less than _____ Dollars ($_____) per monthly
salary; and be it therefore further

        Resolved, That said employment pay rate will allow
new employees to participate in the insurance program following
the ninety-day work performance period."

        There being no further business to come before the meeting, on

motion duly made, seconded, and unanimously carried, the meeting adjourned

at 5:15 p.m.

_____   _____
    Secretary of the Board   Chairman of the Board

Figure 11-6. Minutes of Board of Directors' Meetings. (continued)

PRESS RELEASE

It may be your duty to release information pertaining to the
organization's activities as they develop. Perhaps your boss
dictates the messages by telephone as soon as he possibly can

following the events that he wishes made public, and he instructs
you to relay the message to the local news media.

FROM: Paul R. Nation   DATE: November 20, 19--
         Scholarship Fund Chairman
         National Meeting of "Industry's   (Telephone call
           Search for Students"   verbatim 6:30 p.m.)
         Atlanta, Georgia

         Local office phone: 837-0136

                    FOR IMMEDIATE RELEASE

              INDUSTRIAL CAREER SCHOLARSHIPS

     "Last night the national meeting of 'Industry's Search for

Students' was held at the Shippers Quarters.

     Scholarship Fund Chairman Paul R. Nation, Vice President of the

locally owned Datime Corporation, announced that scholarships will be

awarded to eligible students, beginning next fall.

     The scholarships provide financial assistance to students

seeking a career in industry. To qualify, the student must rank

scholastically in the upper one-third of the class.

     Students interested in applying for a scholarship may write to

Paul R. Nation for an application form. The deadline for accepting

completed applications for next fall's scholarships is January 30."

                         -END-

_____

11-20-   : Telephoned ABCD-TV at 7:05 p.m. Ed Hobbs, News Editor
            took the call and said it would be on tonight's nine
            o'clock newscast.

11-20-   : Telephoned The Newspaper at 7:15 p.m. Marsha Card,
            reporter, took the call; she said it would appear in
            tomorrow morning's edition.

                                                 RAP

              Figure 11-7. Press Release.

After you transcribe "long distance" dictation, make a notation of the time you called in the release and to whom you gave the information.

The illustrated Press Release (Figure 11-7) shows the notations that you would make after the news item is typed and relayed to be released to the public.

When you mail a press release, double space and leave no less than a one-inch margin at the sides and a one and a half inch bottom margin.

In the upper left-hand corner show the origin of the news item.

If more than one page is needed to type the release, indicate "More" within one inch from the bottom of the page. Number succeeding pages in the upper left-hand corner and type key words of the release (Figure 11-8).

```
Page 2 of Industrial Scholarships
```

Figure 11-8.

Place a closing symbol on the last page of the release—"-0-" or "-30-"— a double space following the last line of the release.

Fold the release so that the top portion of the first page is immediately visible when it is pulled from the envelope.

If your firm has the services of a public relations firm, a special form possibly is used to announce business events and other items of public interest.

12

Office Shortcuts

The following paragraphs tell how to utilize time in order to save time.

Centering Sheets of Paper.   If you must center material on paper of various widths and lengths, find the center point by folding the sheet of paper vertically and then gently pinch the center fold at the very edge of the paper. Insert the paper and turn the typewriter cylinder forward until the mark shows directly above the scale. Center the material to be typed from the number that shows directly below the pinched edge (Figure 12-1).

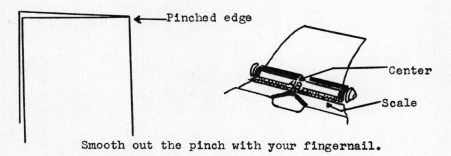

Smooth out the pinch with your fingernail.

Figure 12-1. Quick Centering Method.

Use this same technique when you position two or three typing projects on stencil or ditto masters. Divide the master into the number of typing sections you need, according to the length of material to be typed. If the pinch leaves a mark on the copies, this mark can be used as your guide for cutting the sections on the paper cutter.

A Last Resort.   There was no time to retype a ditto master in order to do away with a correction that turned into a smear that could be measured with a ruler. With the amount of time remaining, the copies would either be decorated with an ink blotch or tape edge marks. The smear was covered with transparent tape, the edges of tape tightly secured to the ditto master—it worked! The copies were distributed without a smear or tape mark.

Correspondence and Filing.   Classify the incoming mail for filing at the time you open it. A pencil notation at the top of the page can be a time saver.

If the sender has failed to enclose material referred to in the letter, make a notation on the letter that enclosures were not included in the letter.

Type letters on a separate sheet of paper if a letter written in longhand is difficult to read. Do not type on the letter itself.

If your boss is involved in several outside activities, sort the mail into separate stacks, one for the company mail and another stack for extra-curricular correspondence.

Attach routing and circulation slips as mail is opened.

Figure discounts on statements as you open mail. Payment of all bills is probably made on a specified date each month. This will eliminate the need to take time to figure discounts before typing checks in payment of the bills later.

Forwarding Mail.   When you send mail (copies only, unless specifically requested by your boss to send originals) to your boss during his out-of-town trips or vacations, number the envelopes consecutively. Transfer the number of the envelope to the carbon copy of your List of Enclosures for your records. This way you will know what items were mailed in the individually numbered envelopes.

Filing Aids.   Typed material or reports that are filed in loose-leaf binders can easily be filed by using the same method for filing general correspondence. Place the most recent record in front of the previously filed material.

Documents and papers that must be folded and stored in file jackets will require less handling if you fold the paper with the typed information on the outside (Figure 12-2).

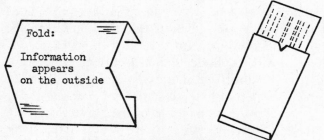

Figure 12-2. Folding Papers for File Jackets.

Papers that are marked and ready for filing may be filed in the "OUT" folder that has been placed in the space where the original folder belongs. Transfer the material from the "OUT" folder to the original file folder as soon as it is returned to the filing cabinet.

Company Manual.   Some of the following material may be considered "pertinent" the next time the company manual is prepared.

- Origin of the company; the services rendered or brief description of products manufactured.
- Observation of local and legal holidays, and the calendar months during which vacations are scheduled.
- Traditional company social functions.
- Payroll distribution dates.
- Rules and regulations for personnel.
- Security precautions and parking facilities.

Revise the material whenever company policies change, if the written guide is affected by any changes made.

Drawing Lines.   Use a hard lead pencil (with a sharpened lead) to draw lines through several thicknesses of paper and carbon. Retrace the pencil lines with an ink pen on the original only. Fasten the packet with paper clips to prevent the paper from sliding out of line.

When you use ink and a ruler for drawing lines, lift the ruler instead of sliding or pulling it away from the line. Fewer smears will appear.

To keep the edge of the ruler clean, pull the ruler across an ink blotter.

Correcting Bound Pages. Pages that are stapled or bound at the top need not be a problem if an error is detected and you are elected to make the correction. Feed a sheet of paper into the typewriter, turn the cylinder forward until the edge of the paper appears. Insert the bottom of the bound page behind the portion of the single sheet that extends above the carriage scale, and roll the cylinder backward to the point of the correction.

Errors that appear on any portion of the bound pages can be easily corrected; and the thickness of the bound material need not cause alarm as long as the weight of the bound pages is supported. Without support, the bound pages may tear away from the one page wrapped around the typewriter cylinder.

Erasing One-Letter Errors. Cut the end of an eraser at an angle after the eraser has been sharpened, but do not sharpen it to a point—keep the end blunt, for strength. Use this eraser for one-letter corrections. Use this angle-cut eraser to erase letter "tails" on carbons.

If the eraser is sharpened to a point, the length of exposed eraser may become so flexible that a break in the eraser will do away with the point in little time.

Erasers and Erasing. Clean two erasers at the same time. Erase one with the other. It works better if the textures are similar.

Use a clean, soft eraser to erase carbon copies. Use a medium textured eraser to erase the error on letterhead or bond paper.

Before you begin erasing, press a soft eraser on the typing error to pull off the surface ink. Use a combination ink-typewriter eraser to remove the remainder of the ink. Shave chalk or lightly rub the chalk stick over the erased area. Set the ribbon control key to stencil position and strike the type bar—this clears some of the chalk from the letter space and makes a neater impression when the inked type bar strikes the erased area. Reset the ribbon control key and type the correct letter.

You may discover a typographical error after you remove the paper from the typewriter. Instead of erasing the paper on a hard surface such as a glass-top desk, cushion the paper with a tablet or other backing. Erasures made on cushioned surfaces appear less torn up than those made when the paper is placed on a hard surface for erasing.

The quality of paper will make a difference in the appearance of erasures.

Multilith Eraser.   Erase ball point ink with a Multilith Eraser (Addressograph-Multigraph Corporation). Rub the mark gently. It may be that several strokes are necessary to erase but the eraser won't break down the paper fiber so readily.

A ball point ink smudge on your nail polish? Erase the mark with a Multilith Eraser.

If you poke yourself with the tip of your ball point pen, gently rub the mark with a Multilith Eraser instead of smearing it with your finger.

Corrections—Plus and Minus One Letter.   If you need to remove one letter from a word, erase the entire word if the word does not contain more than six letters. Reinsert the paper so that the type bar will strike *between* the last two letters of the preceding word. Tap the space bar three times, then type the entire word without using the backspace key or the space bar after the positioning.

Error:	He washed the boat today.
Correction:	He washed the car today.

If you must insert one letter to correct a word, follow the same instructions as above except for the number of times the space bar is to be tapped. After the paper is reinserted so that the type bar will strike between the last two letters of the preceding word, tap the space bar two times, then type the entire word in the same manner described above.

Error:	He washed the car today
Correction:	He washed the boat today.

If your typewriter has a half space key, instructions for removing and inserting type characters are probably outlined in the typewriter manual.

If the correction is a major one and would be the center of

interest on the paper, it may take less time to retype an entire page than to begin erasing an error.

Inserting Carbon Packs. Place the carbon pack between the flap and the back of an envelope. If the paper is 8½ x 11 inches, use a business-size envelope. Turn the typewriter cylinder forward until the envelope clears the paper bail. Remove the envelope and roll the carbon pack into typing position (Figure 12-3).

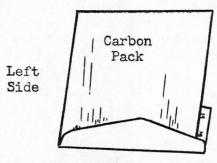

Figure 12-3. Inserting Carbon Packs into Typewriter.

NOTE: The left edge of the envelope must not extend beyond the carbon pack, otherwise the carbon pack will not be positioned on the left side at "0" on the carriage scale.

If the copy sheets begin to pleat, release the Paper Release lever and reset it immediately. With this release, the papers will usually feed through without pleating.

The Lending Act. At times it may be necessary to release documents held in your office to an individual or another office, on a temporary basis. Make up a receipt form for use by your office whenever documents are taken out of the office. Prepare the receipt in duplicate (Figure 12-4). After the borrower signs the receipt, file one copy in the Follow-Up, or Tickler, File; and place the other copy with the remaining papers relating to the borrowed document.

When documents are returned to your office, make a notation to this effect on the copy in the related file, and pull the receipt from the Follow-Up, or Tickler, File for proper disposition.

If more than one document in the same file is removed and the documents will not be returned at the same time, prepare a separate receipt for each item.

```
                        RECEIPT FOR DOCUMENTS

                         (Name of Company)
                          (Department)

Description:  Abstract to Lot 10, Blk 9, First Land Addition,

    Williams County

Purpose:  Transfer of interest

Time Needed:  Approx. two weeks

              Taken for:  CLEAR ABSTRACT COMPANY
                             (Individual or Firm)
                          101 North 42nd Street
                                (Address)
                          439-0999
                              (Telephone No.)
Date                    Document          Date
Taken:  10-9-           Due:  10-23-      Returned:  10-19-


                        RELEASED TO:   Mary Robbin
                                           (Signature)
Officer:  BB
File Attendant:  af
    (Initial)
```

Figure 12-4. Receipt for Documents

The illustration shows information lines on such a receipt and a "returned" notation.

Letter Packs.   Assemble letter packs ahead of time. The rate of use should determine the number of packs you assemble for future needs. An example of when letter packs can save time during heavy typing periods by assembling them ahead of time is given.

> Whenever Mr. A writes a letter to Mr. B, Mr. A needs one copy of the letter for himself and a copy for each Mr. C, Mr. D, and Mr. E. Copies of letters from this pack are distributed to these individuals because they must be kept informed of all transactions.

Therefore, letter packs that would be used each time Mr. A writes to Mr. B would consist of the original sheet plus the number of sheets of carbon paper and copy paper needed for distribution of these copies to the various individuals plus a copy for Mr. A's files.

Store the letter packs in an easily accessible and clean place.

Carbon copies must be legible; therefore, the number of times the carbon paper is used for these packs may be limited to two or three times, depending on the number of copies in each letter pack and the kind of typewriter used. However, do not discard the carbon from these packs. Reuse the carbon, sheet by sheet, for general correspondence when few copies are needed.

Lists: What You Must Do; What Others Do.   Make a list of the things you must do each day. A daily list will enable you to schedule your workday so that no responsibility will be overlooked for each particular day.

Prepare a list of the firm's departments, the services available through each department, and the names of individuals primarily responsible for the department.

Proofing "Original" Identical Letters.   Proofread the first letter typed. Use this as your guide for the next letter. The second letter typed will be your guide for the third letter, and so on. As you type, proofread your guide letter.

Rubber Stamps.   These items can be time savers: date stamps, identification information stamps, and mailing instructions. Notary public commission expiration dates are sometimes affixed to papers with a rubber stamp. If mailing carbon copies of letters is part of everyday's work, perhaps a stamp for affixing this notation to the copies would save time: "Original signed by (*name of individual*)."

Rubber stamps require an occasional cleaning. For clear impressions, use a stiff brush to remove the ink and fiber collections from the cutouts of the stamp.

If you keep rubber stamps in your desk drawer, line the sides and bottom of the drawer with ink blotters or blotter pads. The blotters protect the wood or metal from ink impressions of the rubber stamps.

Smeared Labels?   To avoid smearing typed labels affixed to envelopes, secure the edges of the moistened label to the envelope, turn the envelope face down and apply pressure to the area from the flap side of the envelope.

Use this same technique when labeling file folders. The ink from the typewriter ribbon will not be smeared so readily.

Staggered Totals.   This suggestion comes from *Better Secretaries Series* (Prentice-Hall): Place the first total on the same line as the word "Totals." Type the second total a vertical space below the first column total (under the columnar listing). Continue staggering the remaining totals by turning the typewriter cylinder knob forward one vertical space for each total. Handling large sums in narrow columns is illustrated in Figure 12-5.

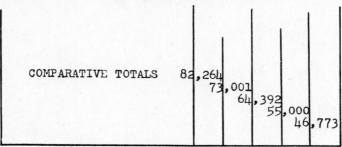

Figure 12-5. Staggered Totals.

Stretching Carbon Paper.   Before you discard sheets of carbon paper, cut those sheets that have the largest borders of unused space into sheets for:

1. typing carbons of 3 x 5 cards
2. typing duplicate copies of your boss' daily appointment list.
3. bank deposit slips—prepare the deposit in duplicate and keep a copy for your records.

Stuffing Envelopes.   Use a ruler to crease several sheets of paper at the same time. In this manner, pre-fold a sizeable stack of sheets before you begin stuffing any envelopes.

Fan the ruler-folded sheets and place the stack to your right, face up, top side down. The stack should look like Figure 12-6.

Place the envelopes, with flap side up, to your left. That stack should look like Figure 12-7.

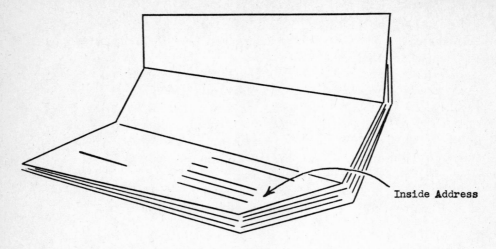

Inside Address

Figure 12-6.

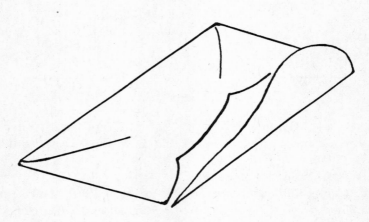

Figure 12-7.

Work with both hands at the same time. With the first finger of the left hand, lift the flap of the envelope as the second finger of the right hand pulls the "top" of the sheet forward. Pull the "top" section of the sheet toward the center section; and as you do this, use your right-hand thumb to push the "bottom" section of the sheet up and over the "top" section (Figure 12-8).

With the folded sheet in your right hand, slide the sheet into the envelope, "bottom" fold first (Figure 12-9).

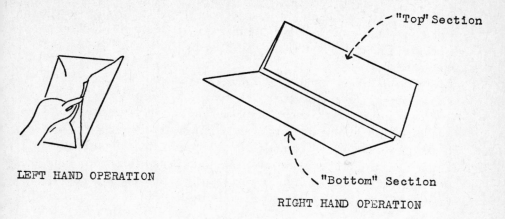

LEFT HAND OPERATION

"Top" Section

"Bottom" Section

RIGHT HAND OPERATION

Figure 12-8.

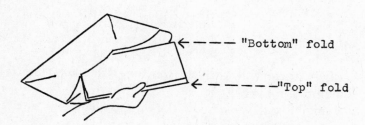

"Bottom" fold

"Top" fold

Figure 12-9.

Leave the envelopes in the original position—flaps up and out. Occasionally press the stack of stuffed envelopes to force out the air. The envelopes are ready for sealing, either by machine or hand.

Subject or *Re* Line Placement.   If the position of the subject or *Re* line confuses you, think this: "Dear Mr. Wise: The subject of this letter is . . . or, Dear Mr. Wise: This letter is in regard to . . . ."

The subject or *Re* line follows the salutation.

Telephone Tips.   Make a list of the subjects you want to discuss on the telephone so that the telephone conversation will be smooth, complete, and brief.

Sometimes a visiting executive or company representative will receive a telephone call at your office. Offer him paper and a pencil for taking notes. Keep a paperweight handy for anchoring paper to make writing easier, since the other hand holds the telephone receiver.

Keep a list of emergency numbers, departments, and frequently called telephone numbers near your telephone for quick reference. Some secretaries keep these numbers under the glass on top of their desks for handy reference, and some secretaries tape the lists to the pull-out counter directly above the top right-hand drawer. If space for these lists is not available in either of these two areas, slide the list of numbers in an inexpensive, unbreakable picture frame and stand the frame on your desk near the telephone. Remove the glass from the frame and replace it with a sheet of plastic. A folding frame can easily be tucked inside the desk at night.

Top-of-the Desk.   Arrange the items you must keep on top of your desk neatly and conveniently. Articles that are used frequently should be placed within easy reach during the day; articles used infrequently should be kept inside the desk in a drawer where there will be little shuffling when you must find them in a hurry.

Clear your desk at the end of the day. Cover your typewriter and put it away at night, if your desk has this feature.

Pencils, erasers, scratch pads, and unfinished paperwork should be placed inside your desk at night. Of the many articles and items you must use during the day, some cannot be put inside your desk—the mail tray, pen holders, and—the telephone.

Your Typewriter.   Center the carriage when the typewriter is not in use.

If you must move the typewriter from one desk to another, center the carriage and lock it in this position by setting the margin stops at this point. This will prevent the carriage from sliding when the typewriter is being transported.

Turn off your electric typewriter when it is not in use.

Read the manual for your typewriter thoroughly. Ask the office equipment store for booklets on the care of your typewriter.

13

Structural Reminder System

The reminder system probably will be seen only by you except during your vacation periods or during sick leave. Temporary help may be requested to fulfill your duties during these absences, or your boss may feel that your work is so well organized that a "substitute" secretary is not necessary during your absence.

A very important letter may be dictated to another department secretary, but all other material may be held for your handling when you return.

The structural reminder system will keep your mind free to concentrate fully on whatever task is at hand. The reminder system is an integral part of a secretary's ability to control the work flow in the office.

Remember the Details "On Paper." For your own use, a reminder form may be made up and duplicated or reproduced (Figure 13-1). It could be labeled a "Reminder," "Pending," or "Follow-Up Note." The form could be reproduced on colored sheets of paper, but be sure to select a color that will not be identical to a more important form used within the office.

If you have in your filing cabinet a reminder file—often called a "tickler" file—consisting of folders for every day of the month, the above form may be useful.

If you have a card file reminder system, information headings on the form could be typed on the cards.

Cards would be more durable than a note-type form if the reminders are handled frequently, or if they become a part of the pertinent business records.

173

```
┌─────────────────────────────────────────────────────────┐
│                     FOLLOW-UP NOTE                        │
│                  (Name of Department)                     │
│                                                           │
│   DUE DATE: 4-20-         SUBJECT: _____   │
│                                                           │
│   REQUESTED BY: (Name)   (Position)   (Address)           │
│                 _____  │
│                                                           │
│   ──────────────────────────────────────────────────     │
│   DETAILS: Wants twelve copies of Form No. 4321           │
│                                                           │
│    sent with supply package next week.                    │
│   DATE OF                REQUEST                          │
│   REQUEST: 4-10-         PROCESSED BY: ar                 │
│                                                           │
│   ACTION TAKEN: Mailed forms w/supplies on 4-16-          │
│                                                           │
└─────────────────────────────────────────────────────────┘
```

Figure 13-1.

One secretary typed her "reminder file" on a sheet of plain bond paper. The duties she performed were attended to on the same day of each month. Opposite the days of the month she listed the specific duty. For example: Opposite the tenth day of the month, this reminder was typed, "Write checks for bills." Opposite the twentieth day of the month, this note was typed, "Mail notices—accounts due last day of month." The periodic duties were also listed on a plain sheet of paper; and the work was completed on schedule.

The reminder form is not intended to be the complete reminder system for an office. The primary purpose of the form is to save time by merely filling in the necessary information. Of course the identification lines may be entirely different from those shown on the form. In addition to saving time by using a form, you can keep your work area neat and avoid discarding an important note by not using just any piece of paper for writing requests which need attention.

It is possible, too, that a spindle will serve your needs just as well as any form or section of a drawer in the filing cabinet, provided the due date is used as your guide when you puncture the reminder.

One Calendar, Two Calendars, Three.   Your desk should be supplied with two calendars—one with space provided to allow for daily appointment scheduling (Figure 13-2); the other calendar

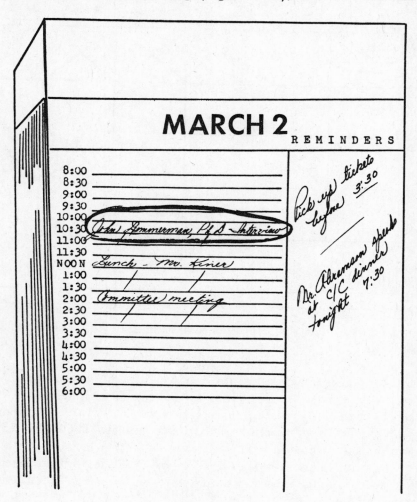

Figure 13-2. Secretary's Desk Calendar for Daily Appointments and Reminders.

should have sufficient space for notations and should show all the days of the month on a single page (Figure 13-3). The latter

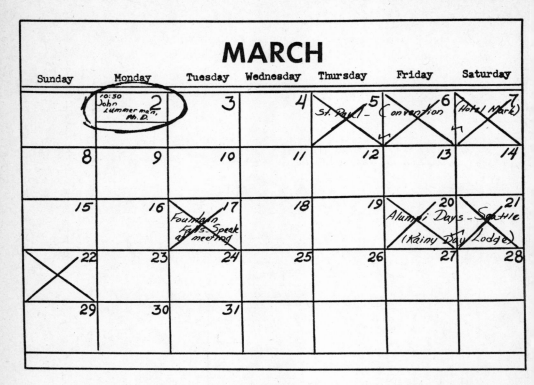

Figure 13-3. Secretary's (Second) Calendar Permits View of Entire Month's Activities.

calendar design would enable you to view the entire month's activities. On this second calendar, list the commitments in the space on the proper dates. This second calendar will be concurrent with the Follow-Up section of the filing cabinet. (The Follow-Up section is illustrated in Figure 13-5.)

The third calendar is your boss' calendar. It should be designed for daily appointments and should have space for brief notations (Figure 13-4).

Illustrations of the secretary's calendars and the boss' calendar show the correlation between all three calendars and the Follow-Up section of the filing cabinet.

All three calendars are marked and a folder has been prepared and placed in chronological order in the Follow-Up section of the filing cabinet.

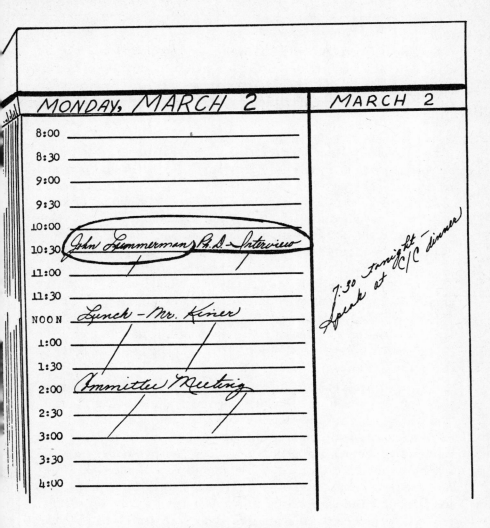

Figure 13-4. Boss' Desk Calendar.

Follow-Up Folders in the Filing Cabinet. Use a section of the filing cabinet drawer as a reminder section and label it, "Follow-Up." Label the folders for future events and file them chronologically. Type the date of the event *first* on the label, followed by the caption describing the event for that particular date.

The Follow-Up section of the filing cabinet might look something like Figure 13-5.

Reminder Form and the Folder.   A reminder form may be clipped to the outside of the folder and filed in the Follow-Up section of the filing cabinet. After the specific details have been attended to, the form may then be filed with the related material in the folder.

A reminder form and folder are shown in Figure 13-6.

The Executive Reminder Note.   You may be asked to return carbon copies of letters to your boss' office for his personal attention.

The facts in the body of a letter dictated and mailed one day may not be as vivid a week later. Type a "Hold" note and attach this note to the carbon copy of the letter. The "Hold" note need not be larger than 4" x 3"; the note should be a brief summary of the letter and points of particular interest to your boss.

At the top of the note, in the upper left-hand corner, type the name of the individual to whom the letter was addressed. Type the date on which the letter was mailed (assuming it was mailed the same day it was dictated) in the upper right-hand corner. In the center of the note, type the word H O L D and the brief recap of the letter, as shown in Figure 13-7.

If you are responsible for opening the mail, and it is assumed that your responsibilities include opening and processing the mail, you will know when the requests have been fulfilled.

You must also remember that the carbon copy of the letter was returned to your boss' office. To avoid panic, should you begin searching for the carbon copy, type yourself a "Follow-Up Note" or type a carbon copy of the "HOLD" note for yourself, and indicate that the carbon copy was returned to your boss at his request, for his personal attention. (This is to serve as a reminder *only;* it is not intended as "evidence" that your boss forgets. Without *your* reminder, you, too, may not have remembered that the carbon copy was returned to the boss' office.)

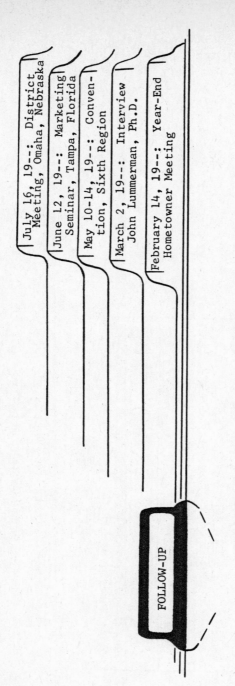

Figure 13-5. Follow-Up Section of Filing Cabinet Drawer.

179

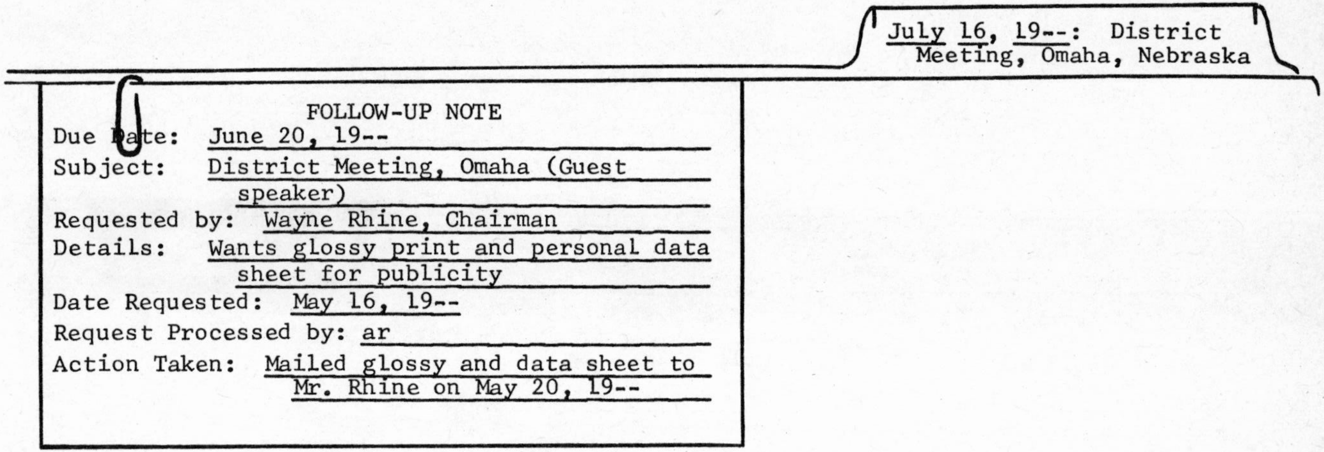

July 16, 19--: District
Meeting, Omaha, Nebraska

FOLLOW-UP NOTE

Due Date: June 20, 19--
Subject: District Meeting, Omaha (Guest
speaker)
Requested by: Wayne Rhine, Chairman
Details: Wants glossy print and personal data
sheet for publicity
Date Requested: May 16, 19--
Request Processed by: ar
Action Taken: Mailed glossy and data sheet to
Mr. Rhine on May 20, 19--

Figure 13-6. Reminder Form Attached to File Folder.

```
(Name of Addressee)    (Date)

        H O L D

Re:  Nathan Grayson
     Mr. Grayson wants to
rent third floor suite.
Holding for reference from
  bank.
```

Figure 13-7. Executive Reminder Note.

14

Filing Finesse

It is important that the files in the office be maintained in order for you to locate papers that are needed by your boss and others who have access to the files. So that you do not waste time searching for filed papers, learn the filing system of the office.

An organization with offices in several locations may have a standard and uniform filing system throughout its many offices. Whatever the filing procedures are, learn the system and follow the filing rules of the office. If you are not sure about the classification of papers to be filed, ask your superior for filing instructions.

Slumped folders and edges of sheets of paper protruding from within the file folders may not be a very impressive sight when you open the file cabinet drawer, but the appearance may not necessarily mean that papers have been filed incorrectly. When you have time, straighten the slumped folders and tap the unevenly placed papers into a neat pile and replace them in the folder from which they are removed. Be very careful to replace the papers in the correct folder.

In a small office the filing system may consist of storing the office papers in a very compact area.

Do not yield to the temptation to scoop papers that are on your boss' desk into neat little piles. The desk may appear to be messy to you but that man who works at that desk usually knows exactly where a piece of paper has been placed or on which tablet a note has been written, and he can probably find it in very little time. Do not remove papers from his office or desk without his permission. Your boss has reasons for not wanting papers removed from his office. Perhaps a former secretary filed far too many letters under "Correspondence," when his own method of keeping track of papers was adequate. He knows he can find the information that he needs.

When your boss feels that you can handle office papers carefully and efficiently, he may ask you for suggestions on organizing those stacks of papers that have been lying on his desk. If he does ask for help in organizing the papers, sturdy folders can be labeled to categorize the various papers. The wording on the folder labels must be appropriate to the contents of the folders. Be sure you check with your boss about correct wordage.

Your conscientiousness in performing your office duties may result in your being approached by your boss for your opinion of the present filing system. If it's adequate, it may be that you periodically clean the file cabinet drawers, replace soiled and torn labels and folders, and add file folders as new names are added to the business.

If the filing system needs some improvement, and your boss expects you to make suggestions, study the various filing systems and discuss these systems with your boss to determine which system is the most suitable one for the office. Changes in the filing system should not be implemented without the approval of your boss.

Four filing systems—alphabetical, numerical, subject, and geographic—are briefly explained with accompanying illustrations.

Before you begin stacking newly labeled folders in the filing cabinet, pull out the filing cabinet drawers for a thorough cleaning and inspection. Remove papers that are crunched behind the drawers. The rod channel at the base of the drawer harbors paper clips, rubber bands and staples that have been released from filed papers. Salvage the reusable rubber bands and clips. Periodically wipe the drawers to remove the minute paper fibers that drift to the bottom. The filing cabinet should be included in your office cleaning.

Alphabetical Filing.   The principle used in alphabetical filing is: File papers according to the letters in the alphabet. Guides are printed from A through Z. File folders are labeled with the brief caption describing the material that is to be placed in the respective folders. Behind the captioned folders, aligned alphabetically, place a miscellaneous folder for each letter in the alphabet. In the lettered miscellaneous folders, store papers that, at the time of filing have no specific relationship to the already captioned folders. As soon as five or more papers are related, label a folder specifically for that exchange of correspondence.

The first illustration of a filing cabinet drawer is an arrangement of folders labeled with personal names and names of organizations arranged in alphabetical order (Figure 14-1).

Color may be used to facilitate filing and finding papers. Color tends to draw interest to the duty of filing, if in the past it has not been a favorite office task. However, just to add color for the sake of color may not increase filing efficiency—color must have some distinction within the filing system used.

A color key should identify the various classifications of filed material. For the illustration, color is used to distinquish one classification of personnel from the others (Figure 14-2).

If you use a color key it should become a part of the procedures manual discussed in Chapter 17. An identical chart should be placed in your desk, since folders probably will be prepared at your desk. Or it may be placed in the forepart of the filing cabinet drawer if this is more convenient.

The second filing cabinet drawer illustration shows the labeled folders filed alphabetically with an identifying color assigned to each folder name (Figure 14-3).

Geographic Filing.   Possibly the most efficient record-keeping method for companies operating throughout the adjacent states and perhaps abroad is the geographic filing system. Geographic filing may be essential when business activity necessitates territorial divisions or area representation. Division offices are maintained to govern business activities within defined boundary lines. As an example only, assume that the major land division titles serve as file guides; divide the major territories again, this time by states within the regional jurisdiction; subdivide the states into cities or counties (Figure 14-4).

Turn to the map (Figure 14-5) which shows the regional boundaries and color key. Comparing the map with the illustration of the filing cabinet drawer, notice that the regions are the guides in the filing cabinet drawer, the states are the subdivisions, followed

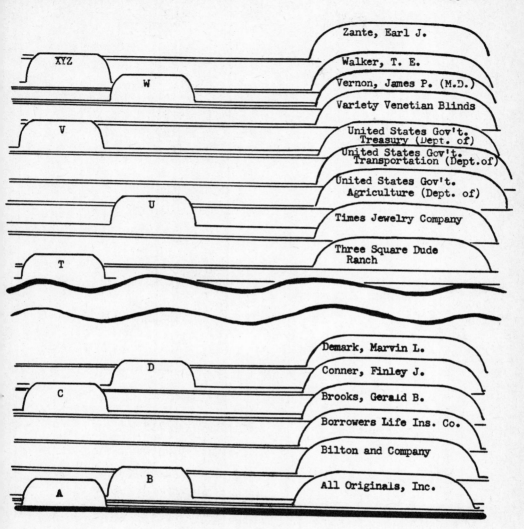

Figure 14-1. Filing Cabinet Drawer: File Folders Arranged Alphabetically.

by the individual folders. The folders represent cities where branch offices are located. (The directional descriptions on the map are strictly for the purpose of illustrating the geographic filing system.)

The regional color codes could be carried to the filing cabinet. All folders filed in the Southern Region section of the filing

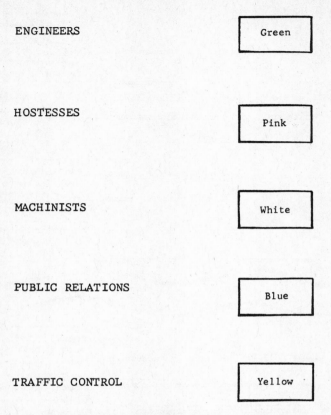

ENGINEERS

HOSTESSES

MACHINISTS

PUBLIC RELATIONS

TRAFFIC CONTROL

Green

Pink

White

Blue

Yellow

Figure 14-2. Color Key for Personnel Classification.

cabinet would be affixed with brown tone folder labels. Folders filed in the Pacific Coast Region section would be grey-labeled, and yellow labels would be used for the folders filed in the New England Region section of the filing cabinet.

In any office, the primary concern is filing efficiency. If color association aids in filing accuracy and office efficiency, perhaps it should be considered.

What appears to be a more complicated filing system but perhaps more accurate is the use of numbers along with the geographic filing system. If branch offices are satellite operations of regional offices and similar reports are sent to the Home Office, a number would be assigned to each region.

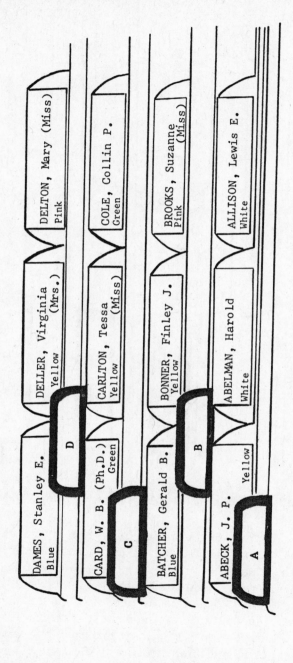

Figure 14-3. Filing Cabinet Drawer: File Folders Arranged Alphabetically with Color Identity.

187

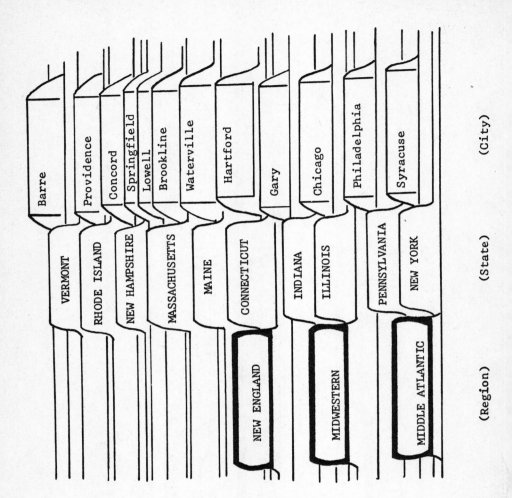

Figure 14-4. Filing Cabinet Drawer: Geographic Filing System.

The map (Figure 14-5a) is divided into seven regions. Using the same regional boundaries and all other divisions, the map is also marked with a number for each region. The Middle Atlantic Region is number "1," Midwestern Region is number "2," New England Region is "3," and so on according to the alphabetical listing of the regions outlined on the map.

Generally, business operations are managed by personnel in district, or regional, and branch offices. The area under regional

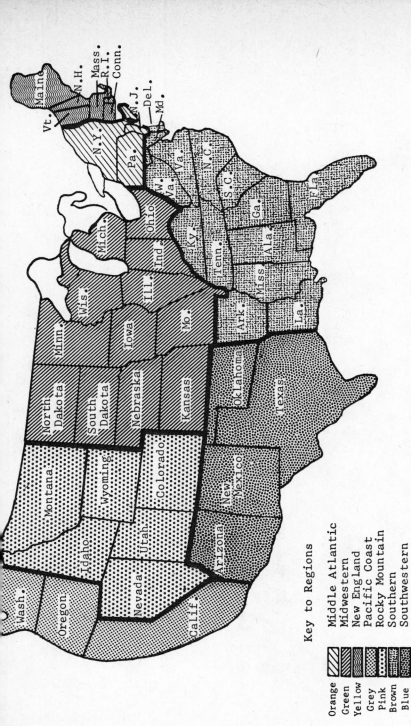

Key to Regions

Orange	Middle Atlantic
Green	Midwestern
Yellow	New England
Grey	Pacific Coast
Pink	Rocky Mountain
Brown	Southern
Blue	Southwestern

Figure 14-5. Map Showing Code Numbers and Regional Boundaries for Geographic Filing.

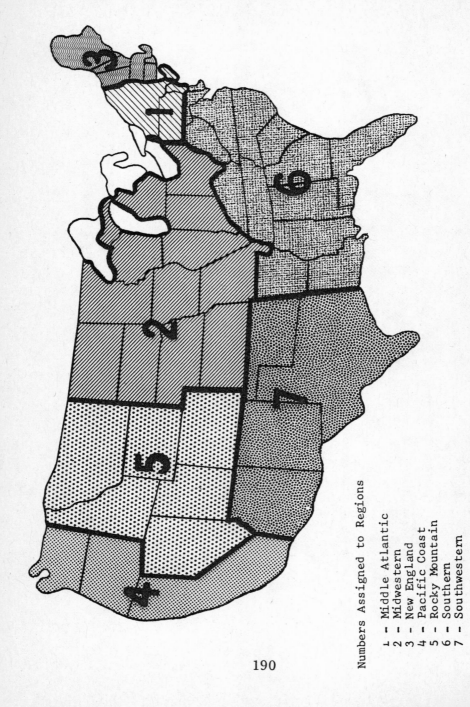

Figure 14-5a. Map Showing Code Numbers and Regional Boundaries for Geographic Filing.

Numbers Assigned to Regions

1 – Middle Atlantic
2 – Midwestern
3 – New England
4 – Pacific Coast
5 – Rocky Mountain
6 – Southern
7 – Southwestern

authority is divided into branch offices, and these, too, are assigned numbers. For example, all branch offices in the Middle Atlantic Region would have the number "1" as part of the branch code number. Syracuse, New York accordingly is in Region One; that branch office has been coded 11. Philadelphia, Pennsylvania would be coded as also being in Region One and it is the second branch office in that region; the code number would be 1-2 or 12.

The Midwestern Region is Region Two. All branch offices in that region would begin with the number "2," plus the number assigned to the branch office. If there are two branch offices in Region Two, the office numbering would be 2-1, or 21, and 2-2, or 22.

The same numbering procedure would be applied to the remaining regions.

Subject Filing.   Learn the terminology within the office. It will be to your advantage when you must file and locate papers in the subject file.

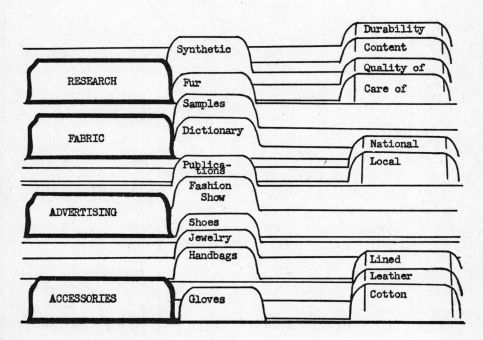

Figure 14-6. Filing Cabinet Drawer: Subject Filing.

In subject filing, the file guides and folders represent things, kinds or types of things, organizations, and people. All guides, subdivisions, and folders are filed in alphabetical order.

A simple subject file arrangement is shown in Figure 14-6.

Numeric Filing.   In the numeric filing system, every piece of paper that is to become part of the office records must be assigned the appropriate number. Numbered folders are arranged consecutively. The assigned number must be written on every piece of correspondence. If it is your responsibility to see that all papers and folders are in proper order, although other employees are at liberty to remove folders from the filing cabinet, the numeric filing system may make your work easier. It may not reduce the time it takes to search for the missing folder, but you will be able to more readily detect empty folder spaces in the file. Because of the consecutive number arrangement, "25" always follows "24" and number "24" always follows number "23." In the alphabetical filing system, a folder for Bales may not always follow the folder for Bade. A new customer named Bagg would separate Bade and Bales.

The first example of a numeric filing system will be an imaginary insurance firm. The first customer to whom a policy has been issued is Henry G. Post. The second customer is William Bell. (Folder numbers begin with "1.")

An Alphabetical Directory is maintained as policies are issued. The directory, which is the referral list for obtaining the insured's complete file, lists pertinent information and is color coded. Refer to Figures 14-7 and 14-8.

The Alphabetical Directory should be mounted in a convenient place, preferably between your desk and the filing cabinet. The concise information is typed on one-line strips of flexible card-weight paper. These strips are inserted into narrow transparent protectors which are then anchored in alphabetical position.

The directory serves a second purpose. The color code serves as an alert signal for the number of premiums due for any particular month. Each month is color coded; one color for each of the twelve months. As premiums are paid, a new strip indicating the month that the next premium is due would be reinserted alphabetically.

ALPHABETICAL DIRECTORY

POLICYHOLDER'S NAME	MAILING ADDRESS	INSURANCE	PREMIUM DUE	FOLDER NO.
Allison, Theodore	21 Mild Meadow	Auto	June, 19-- Green	19
Archer, Mark	15 E. 21st St.	Auto	Oct., 19-- Brown	8
Ball, David	1801 So. Pierce	Commercial	Jan., 19-- Yellow	21
Bell, William	376 Wesley Way	Homeowners	Febr., 19-- Pink	2
Brock, Marvin	1765 Mason Pl.	Auto	Dec., 19-- Blue	20
Camer, J. E.	5800 N. Camel	Homeowners	March, 19-- Orange	36

Post, Henry G.	818 West Nile	Commercial	Febr., 19-- Pink	1
Redder, Alvin B.	109 Broadway	Health	June, 19-- Green	5
Smythe, Calvin C.	4352 Ark Avenue	Homeowners	May, 19-- Violet	6
Timble, E. L.	2169 Northwood	Auto	Nov., 19-- Grey	3

Figure 14-7. Alphabetical Directory.

Policy numbers may also be typed on the strips. Complete details, of course, would be obtained by pulling the numbered folder whenever necessary.

Many factors within the office may determine the necessity for a policy register. Column headings such as those shown may be sufficient in a small office. Record the numbers consecutively and whatever other data is required by the office (Figure 14-9).

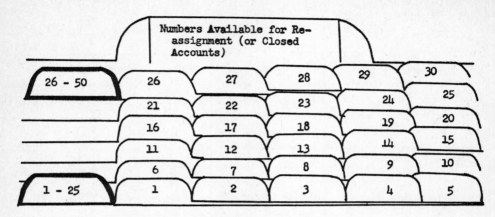

Figure 14-8. Filing Cabinet Drawer: Numeric Filing.

POLICY REGISTER

Policy Number	Insured	Date Issued	Agent
1001	Henry G. Post	1-14-	G. Billings
1002	William Bell	1-18-	H. Mintel
1003	E. L. Timble	1-20-	T. Stone
1004	Void	1-20-	--- T.S.

Figure 14-9. Policy Register.

In addition to the numeric filing cabinet and the Alphabetical Directory, the office must have filing space for inactive records. These records would be filed alphabetically. As the customer's name is removed from the company's active records, the papers relating to the account are transferred to the alphabetical file. The name is removed from the Alphabetical Directory; and the folder number may be assigned to another customer, unless the nature of the business prohibits reassigning numbers.

A second numeric filing system covered and illustrated briefly is only one department of a business. The letter used with the number will designate the department. In this case, "T" represents Trust Department. Numbers are assigned consecutively as accounts are opened. Prepare a register of assigned numbers. The design and method of recording will depend on office needs. A simple number register is shown in Figure 14-10.

ACCOUNT NUMBER REGISTER	
Account Number	Name
T-301	Bernard Hill
T-302	James Brown
T-303	Sam Winter
T-304	G. Paul Garfield
T-305	Eric Snider

Figure 14-10.

A color code could be added to identify the type of service rendered. If there are five types of services performed, you would need five different colors.

In addition to listing the type of service rendered for each account, include the date the account was opened (Figure 14-11).

ACCOUNT NUMBER REGISTER

Account Number	Name	Type of Service	Date Opened
T-301	Bernard Hill	Agent	2-5-
T-302	James K. Brown	Administrator	2-15-
T-303	Sam Winter	Executor	2-15-
T-304	G. Paul Garfield	Agent	3-2-
T-305	Eric Snider	Administrator	4-6-
T-306	George B. Crete	Guardian	4-7-
T-307	Lynn Selton	Executor	5-28-
T-308	Gerald Eiselmann	Trustee	6-2-

Figure 14-11.

Place all papers relating to the respective accounts in the numbered folders. Add to the folder labeled with the account number a brief description of the contents. Individual account numbers serve as file guides.

Figure 14-12 shows a portion of the file drawer indicating that a number of specifically labeled folders are necessary for every account serviced by the firm.

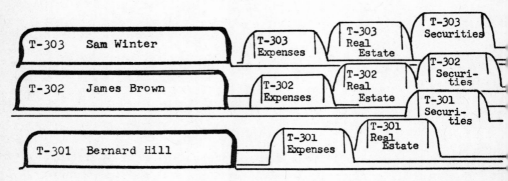

Figure 14-12. Numeric Filing Arrangement for Single Account with Several Folders.

Card Index.   Begin a card index, or file, as soon as the department is functioning. Type a card for every individual or organization that has properly requested the specific services available. The nature of the business and the type of service requested may make it necessary to provide safekeeping space. Such deposited documents could then be retained in an alphabetical filing cabinet until circumstances require conversion to the numeric file.

Prepare cards for folders retained in the alphabetical file. Letter "A" indicates that the folder is filed in the alphabetical filing cabinet. Record the name of the depositor, the documents deposited, the date, and the type of service to be rendered. Sample file cards are shown in Figure 14-13.

Cards prepared for the numbered accounts handled by the department will show the date the account was opened, the name under which the service is being rendered, the type of service, and the account number. (When the names on the cards filed alphabetically become active accounts, the original file card can

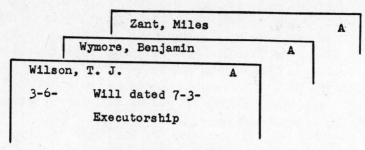

Figure 14-13. Card Index.

then be marked with the assigned account number and all other information that must be added to it.)

File cards with account numbers will look like Figure 14-14.

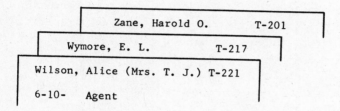

Figure 14-14. Card Index.

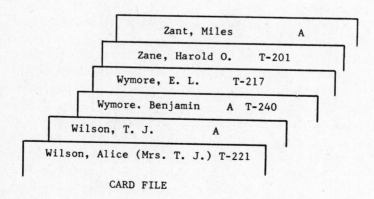

Figure 14-15. Card Index.

The cards should be filed alphabetically. The card file, housing both sets of cards, will appear as shown in Figure 14-15.

The Call for Filed Material.   Your boss or other authorized employee may call for a folder while pondering a situation at the wall map. He may ask for it by number. You could then go directly to the filing cabinet and pull the folder if the company records are filed numerically.

If a visitor stops in the office to check a recent or anticipated business venture, you may be asked to pull the visitor's folder. This time your boss may ask for "Mr. Wood's" folder. Unless you have the number of Mr. Wood's folder memorized, it would be necessary to check the alphabetical list or card file for the correct folder number before leafing through the filing cabinet drawers.

Another arrangement associated with numerical filing is the chart or catalog. The chart or catalog may be divided by an alphabetical listing of the items appearing on the chart or in the catalog. From the chart or catalog you would be able to find the item number.

Office requirements for filing vary. Stationery and office equipment dealers have a variety of serviceable filing systems. The system that serves your office needs is the right one.

Filing Odds and Ends.   Every item placed in the filing cabinet need not and perhaps should not be trimmed or folded to fit the folder considered standard for your office. Special envelopes and file jackets should be used for material of special interest not related to the function of the office. These items should be placed in a separate filing cabinet drawer and properly labeled.

Cross-Reference Filing.   Correspondence, according to the content, may be correctly filed in one folder or another; but to elimate guesswork, a cross-reference sheet will aid in filing, and locating, the specific paper.

A cross-reference sheet might be handy in the following instance: At the annual stockholders meeting, the corporation had a guest speaker for the program. The speaker was Wesley Byrde. Mr. Byrde is well known in the area; he is retired and travels extensively. Time allows him to relate these interesting experiences to various groups.

The correspondence relating to the stockholders meeting would be filed in the stockholder meeting folder. Following the stockholders meeting, the corporation reimburses Mr. Byrde for his travel expenses and a stipulated fee. Correspondence with Mr. Byrde would be part of the papers relating to the stockholders meeting and, therefore, would be filed in the stockholders meeting folder also.

CROSS-REFERENCE SHEET

NAME: BYRDE, Wesley   DATE: March 10, 1968
One Ponder Plaza
Helena, Montana

RE: Mr. Byrde was featured speaker at the twenty-fifth annual stockholders meeting on March 4, 1968.

S E E
SUBJECT: MEETINGS, ANNUAL: Stockholders

ar   (Initials to identify file attendant)

Figure 14-16. Cross-reference Sheet.

A cross-reference sheet would be made up and filed in the "B" (for Byrde) folder.

Figure 14-16 is a sample cross-reference sheet showing that the correspondence was filed according to *subject* matter (Meetings, Annual: Stockholders), with the cross-reference sheet filed in "B" miscellaneous.

Overseer of the Filing Cabinet.   The kind of business, the size of the business, and the number of employees may regulate the accessibility to the material in the filing cabinets.

In some businesses, the filing cabinets may be the center of activity; and the length of time that a folder is out of the filing cabinet may not necessitate a written request for filed material. If the filing cabinets are centrally located and ten people are free to pull any folder whenever the folder is needed, business activity may be hindered if every one of the ten individuals took the time to write his request just as a formality.

The distinction of overseer of the filing cabinet in this business arrangement may carry with it the responsibility of seeing to it that all folders and material pulled from the filing cabinet during the day are refiled at the end of each day. Making the material available to the authorized people may be more of a responsibility than knowing which of the ten people has a certain folder.

Larger organizations may not allow such a liberal procedure in a filing cabinet center. An employee's position in the organization may have some bearing on how quickly one can obtain the material requested. However, if the material requested is not in use, it usually can be obtained without undue delay, by meeting the file attendant's requirements for releasing filed material.

A sign-out sheet may be sufficient for recording the material released, should your office files contain material that has been lent to others in the organization.

Filed material removed from a filing cabinet may be recorded on a form similar to Figure 14-17, designated as a Sign-Out Sheet.

There are other systems to employ when releasing filed material. Every office should have some system for releasing any filed material, whether it be out of necessity or preference.

Prepare File Folders for Durability and Neatness.   Setting up the filing system may take some time and may be a chore, some of the time; but when you finally have it arranged you will be proud

SIGN-OUT SHEET

(Name of Department)

Sheet
Number: 34

MATERIAL RELEASED	DATE RELEASED	BORROWER'S SIGNATURE	MATERIAL RETURNED	
			Date	File Clerk

Figure 14-17. Sign-Out Sheet.

of your accomplishment. Filing no longer will be the first duty you would eliminate if you were asked what one area of office work you would like to abolish.

Arrange your files neatly. After you have them arranged, keep the folders in neat order. You can and should be proud of your files. Your boss, too, will be proud and pleased when you provide efficient service whenever he requests filed papers.

Preparing the Folder for the Filing Cabinet.   Select a label in a color that will harmonize with the colors in your office. The color, or colors, should be selected with the file folder tab labels and guides in mind.

After you have typed the folder label and affixed it to the folder tab, reinforce the folder tab and label with a strip of transparent tape. This helps keep the label clean, as well as reducing the number of times new labels must be typed.

Crease the folder on the indented line at the bottom of the folder. This allows the folder to rest on the "square," and prevents the folders from falling forward; it eliminates the "slumped" look in the filing cabinet.

Usually there are three indented lines to indicate where the creases can be made. The number of sheets to be filed in any one folder will be your guide for creasing the indented line. As the material for filing increases the need for additional space in any one folder, crease the second line or the third line.

Figure 14-18 represents the indented lines on a file folder and how the folder appears after one of the indented lines has been creased.

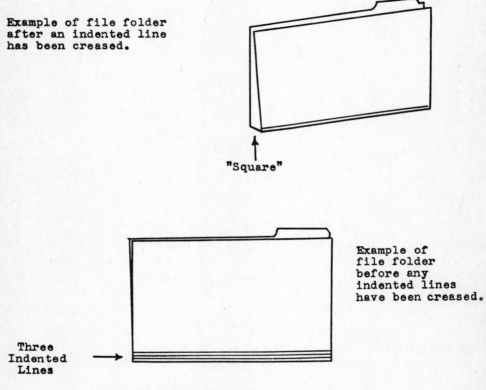

Example of file folder
after an indented line
has been creased.

"Square"

Example of
file folder
before any
indented lines
have been creased.

Three
Indented
Lines

Figure 14-18. File Folders with Capacity-Indicator Lines.

Paper Clips in File Folders.   The only time paper clips should be used to hold related papers together in a file folder is when you know that additional papers are to be filed within a very short period of time. Paper clips should not be used as permanent fasteners for inactive material. As soon as all related papers are assembled in the file, staple them together.

Stapling Carbon Copies.   File copies are usually typed on onionskin or some other lighter weight paper. Before stapling another piece of paper to the file copy, reinforce the area of the file copy where the staple will be lodged. Sometimes staples must be removed because only the file copy has been requested for one reason or another. The file copy, when it is returned for filing, must again be stapled to the related papers. The file copy can easily and very quickly become shredded without some reinforcement.

Figure 14-19 illustrates the point made in the preceding paragraph.

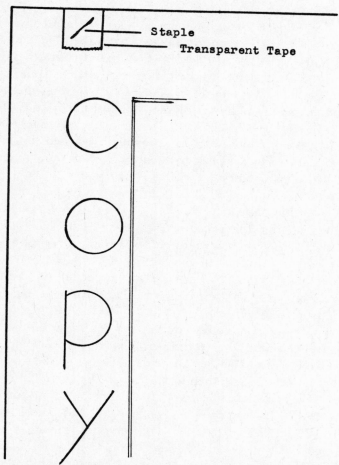

Figure 14-19. Reinforcement for Carbon Copies to Be Stapled.

Folder Placement in the Filing Cabinet.   Allow at least ten to fourteen inches in each drawer of the filing cabinet for future expansion. This means that when you distribute the file folders throughout the filing cabinet, none of the drawers should be filled to capacity.

This extra space may be needed within a short time; but perhaps before your filing cabinet reaches its capacity for holding papers, it may be time to transfer or discard some of the papers.

The file expansion allowance will save juggling the outside filing cabinet labels and moving folders from one drawer to another unnecessarily.

Label the Filing Cabinet Drawers.   Label the filing cabinet drawers to correspond with the arrangement of the file guides.

File Cabinet Directory.   After you have arranged the file folders in the order that is best for your office, type a File Cabinet Directory. The directory should be typed in duplicate, and it should include a sketch of the filing cabinets. The original Directory should be placed in a permanent place in the filing cabinet, or placed in the procedures manual discussed in Chapter 17. A copy should be available for your boss, even though he may prefer not to keep a copy in his office.

List every file guide and folder caption in the order that they appear in the filing cabinet.

A sketch of the filing cabinet, as the drawer labels would appear, and the file cabinet directory arrangement appear in Figure 14-20.

On Your Mark—File!   Mark on the upper left-hand corner, with pencil, on every letter, report, or other document, where the correspondence will be filed.

. When you have completed your marks for filing, arrange the papers to be filed according to the alignment of the folders.

Refer to your File Cabinet Directory (Figure 14-20) when in doubt about the marking, then look through the most appropriate folder to verify the marking; but never file the correspondence until you know exactly what the subject matter is and how it is related to the activity of the company for which you are working, and more particularly, what it demands from your office.

Top Secret!   There will be some papers that your boss will

FILE CABINET DIRECTORY

FILE GUIDE	FOLDER CAPTION
A	Arranged Alphabetically
B	Brief Caption
C	Continue Listing Through "Z"
D	Do Not Forget to Use Different Colored Labels for Folders that are to be Filed in Your Boss' Office

FILE CABINET DRAWERS (AS LABELED)

CORRESPONDENCE FOLLOW-UP A through B	DRILLING CONTRACTS 1968 through 19__
CORRESPONDENCE C through E	DRILLING CONTRACTS 1966 through 1967

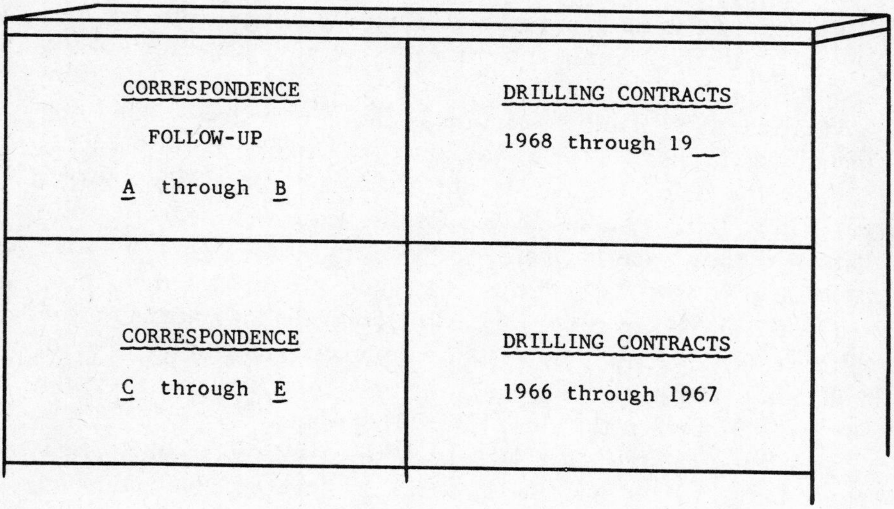

Figure 14-20. File Cabinet Directory, File Cabinet Drawers (as Labeled).

want filed in his desk filing drawer, or in some other special file in his office. Probably only the two of you (or maybe just your boss) will have access to this private file.

You probably will be asked to find a paper that previously had been designated as "confidential," and which was filed in your boss' office file. It may be good practice to prepare a duplicate or "mock" folder that will contain only cross-reference sheets, to indicate what material is filed in his office file.

The File Cabinet Directory should include a list of the folders that are retained in your boss' office. The labels should be a different color from those in your office, to avoid "losing" the folders by placing them in the general office filing cabinet instead of in the boss' private file.

Transferring Filed Material.   Transfer filed material according to company policy.

An established firm may have specified months for transferring files. Some firms transfer filed material at the close of the fiscal year. Companies which have not been in operation long may transfer filed material when business activity warrants disposing outdated papers.

An Empty File Basket!   Setting up the filing system can be a special challenge. Time and thought are necessary for such a project.

What the filing cabinet contains is another challenge. Although many secretaries breathe a sigh of relief when the file basket is empty, the filing cabinet is not a burial ground for another company's letterhead simply because the correspondence is up to date or the letter has been answered.

From time to time, pull the folders and leaf through the papers; scan or read the material in the folders. This may acquaint you with correspondents—you will be able to recognize names of individuals and companies when the telephone rings and the caller identifies himself or the company he represents.

The filing cabinet should be an active part of the business. It could be identified as a special compartment where customers are sheltered and protected, not shoved in a "Manila" tomb.

15

Business Meetings

Business meetings can be any kind of meeting or many kinds of meetings—department heads meet, special committees meet, standing committees meet, stockholders meet, board of directors meet, and personnel assemble for meetings.

Learn how much "meeting" activity takes place within the company and how this activity affects your work and that of your boss. Read the company bylaws. Find out how many members serve on the various committees, the number of committees and the functions of each, the committee chairmen, the number of stockholders, and the names of members serving as directors.

Find out how many times a year the various committees meet, and where the meetings are held. If you are responsible for notifying committee members that a meeting has been scheduled, you should also have access to the material concerning your responsibilities, such as a list of all the committee members and their mailing addresses and telephone numbers, and a list of the stockholders. If your work area is not equipped with the "efficiency implements," ask for them.

Regularly Scheduled Meetings.   If time is automatically set aside for weekly meetings, block off this time on both your desk appointment calendar and your boss' desk calendar. Block off this time for the entire year, if the meetings are set up for that length of time. Meetings held this frequently usually involve personnel with executive-level responsibilities within the company. These meetings are informal meetings.

207

Taking notes at these meetings consists of recording only the main topics discussed, unless you are instructed to record a portion of the meeting verbatim. The minutes of the meetings should be transcribed and distributed to the committee members promptly. Discussion topics may require the action of some members on the committee within an allotted time and prior to another meeting.

If attendance records are kept, one form may serve your needs for all meeting attendance records. If you have access to a duplicating machine, a form could be set up for design only, and the headings added to correspond with the respective committees, and committee member names written in. (Figure 15-1 was designed for weekly meetings.)

Special Committee Meetings.   The day of the month may vary for special committee meetings held periodically. Business activity may dictate what day of the month certain committees will meet.

The telephone may serve as the official notice of the special committee meetings. Or you may have time to notify the committee members by mail. (Many committees are comprised of individuals who are not on the payroll and who do not live in the same city—these individuals are sometimes shareowners or are personally interested in an organization.)

Mark the calendars as soon as the meeting date has been established. If notices were mailed, retain a copy for the file.

Informal meetings may commence in your boss' office. Make arrangements to have chairs delivered to his office, provide ashtrays, scratch pads, pencils; slip an extra box of matches to your boss for his guests who come without them. Coffee or tea service will depend on your boss' wishes.

Board of Directors' Meetings.   Learn what method of communication is to be used to notify members of the board that a meeting is scheduled. Who readies the board meeting room? Are vouchers to be prepared for the directors who attend the meetings? What are the directors to receive as fees, and is there any allowance for mileage? You will also want to know if checks to the directors are to be distributed as soon as the meeting adjourns or if they are to be mailed at a later date. Mailing lists

COMMITTEE MEMBER LIST
and
MEETING DATE RECORD

(Name of Committee)

NAME OF MEMBER	JANUARY				FEBRUARY				MARCH					APRIL				MAY				JUNE				
	6	13	20	27	3	10	17	24	3	10	17	24	31	7	14	21	28	5	12	19	26	2	9	16	23	30
ALEXANDER, Paul	x	x	x	x	-	x	x																			
BETTMAYER, Earl	-	x	x	x	x	x	x																			
CETLAU, M. Frank	x	x	x	x	x	x	x																			
DIDIER, J. L.	x	x	x	x	x	x	x																			
EVANS, Maurice	x	x	x	x	x	-																				
FINZELLI, A. M.	x	x	x	x	-	-	x																			

Figure 15-1.

209

must be complete and up to date. The agenda—find out whose responsibility this is.

Stockholders' Meetings.   Stockholders usually meet once a year and within several weeks following the close of the fiscal year. Corporation policy may prescribe that an affidavit be prepared stating that the meeting notices were mailed on a specified date.

If a dinner precedes the meeting, arrangements for dining facilities must be made; the menu must be planned. Reports for distribution must be prepared and printed. When will dividend checks be distributed—before or after the meeting? Who prepares the dividend checks? Who is in charge of the ballot preparation and printing? Has a counting board been selected? Will there be a guest speaker? Who is responsible for these arrangements: the speaker's travel and hotel reservations?

Your major participation in the meeting may be the recording of the minutes. You would be seated at the head table perhaps.

Meeting Notice and Proxy.   The announcement of the stockholders' meeting may vary. In a very small company, each stockholder would no doubt receive an individually typed notice. Printed notices are usually prepared and mailed when the stockholder list exceeds the production facilities within the office.

Check with your boss about placing the meeting notice in the newspaper. This may be required procedure for some businesses.

Stockholders who do not plan to attend the meeting are usually requested to authorize another person or "agent" to vote his shares. The stockholder voting power is passed to the designated person in the form of a proxy.

It is not unusual for the meeting notice to be printed on one side of a card with the Proxy form printed on the reverse side.

Figure 15-2 shows a Meeting Notice-Proxy card.

The Full Day.   An entire day may be set aside for entertaining the stockholders as well as reviewing business activities of the past fiscal year.

A coffee hour may officially signal the day's beginning for the stockholders. During this hour entertainment may be provided by a small singing group. The morning event probably would be held in one of the city's newer and larger buildings, with facilities to

Stockholder Meeting Notice on Front of Card

(Name of Company)

NOTICE

The annual meeting of the stockholders of Highland Hills Corporation is to be held Tuesday, March 9, 19--, at ten o'clock in the morning, at the Home Office in Boston, Massachusetts. You are entitled and invited to attend this meeting as a stockholder. If you are unable to attend this meeting, you may appoint a proxy to vote your shares. The proxy form printed on the reverse side of this Notice will, upon completion and receipt, be recognized as your wish to be represented by the proxy named.

Proxy Form on Reverse Side of Card

PROXY

I, the undersigned and shareholder of Highland Hills Corporation hereby constitute and appoint B. A. Hight, Thomas C. Kare, and L. W. Wills, directors of the Corporation, as my proxy to act for me at the annual meeting on Tuesday, March 9, 19--, with full power of substitution or revocation and at any adjournments thereof to act for me with the full power and authority that I would possess if I were personally present.

This Proxy shall remain in force, unless withdrawn by the shareholder, only until final adjournment of this annual meeting of the Highland Hills Corporation.

Dated and signed this _____ day of _____, 19--.

_____
(Shareholder)

Figure 15-2. Stockholder Meeting Notice and Proxy Form.

comfortably accommodate large groups, particularly when spouses are invited to share the day.

An hour or two perhaps would separate the official beginning of the day from the business session, which sometimes is preceded by a midday dinner.

Preparatory work begins several weeks or months before the important day set aside for the stockholders. Arrangements for all events scheduled during the day must be discussed, planned, and confirmed.

Reply Cards.   Stockholder attendance might be predicated on a percentage basis by using previous meeting records as the guide. Reply cards inserted in the envelope with the meeting notice might provide a more accurate figure. The card requests each stockholder to indicate whether or not he plans to attend any of the events scheduled for the day. Invitations extended to the spouse of the stockholder increase the need for attendance estimates.

The reply cards are used to compute the approximate number of guests for each session. Final arrangements for the coffee hour, dinner, and meeting can then be made from the response.

If your office pays the return postage on the reply cards, include this expense in the planning.

Some stockholders will verbally respond instead of returning the card by mail. Perhaps they will stop at your desk or telephone your office and say something, such as, "I'll be there—all day."

Figure 15-3 shows what information might appear on the reply card.

```
              Highland Hills Corporation

                  Stockholders Day

                   March 9, 19--

      Please reserve the number of places indicated
      below:

             _____ for the Coffee Hour

             _____ for the Dinner and Meeting


                   _____
                        (Stockholder)
```

Figure 15-3. Reply Card.

To compute the replies from the cards and the verbal replies, prepare a sheet for tabulation. It may not be necessary to keep records on the will-not-attends for the nonbusiness events, but all figures may be important for the stockholder meeting record.

A sheet for tabulating the replies might be similar to Figure 15-4.

STOCKHOLDER REPLIES FOR MARCH 9, 19--			
COFFEE HOUR	DINNER	M E E T I N G	
(Yes's Only)		Yes	No
4	2	4	o
2	2	4	2
6	4	6	2
total: 2-14 12	8	14	2
5	5	5	-
8	6	8	2
total: 2-18 13	11	27	2

Figure 15-4. Tabulated Sheet for Scheduled Events.

Following the annual meeting, find out if highlights of the meeting are to be relayed to news media.

The Guest Speaker.   Treat the guest speaker with the same courtesy after he delivers his speech that you extended to him in the invitation to appear as guest speaker. See to it that transportation is provided for him while he is in the city. Doublecheck the podium to be sure a pitcher of water and glasses are provided for the speaker.

Write a thank-you letter to the guest speaker following the meeting, and include the honorarium and any travel expenses which the speaker incurred for his trip to your city.

Hint

Ask your boss if he usually sends a letter to the
stockholders who could not attend the meeting. Would
the letter be a brief account of the business activity for
the year? Would dividend checks be enclosed in the
letter? Printed reports and the agenda—would copies of
these be included among the mailed items?

16

Paper Cushions for the Business Trip

By using *effort* as the chief apparatus coupled with the "knack" for handling details, you can anticipate the material your boss will need and want in his briefcase. The "cushioning" that you provide for your boss while he travels will consist of the papers you assemble for his trip. The papers and the details that you have attended to prior to his departure must represent the most efficient planning.

The following details will require your attention immediately upon confirmation of any scheduled appointments out of town. *Travel arrangements* and *overnight accommodations* must be made; assemble the *correspondence* needed during his trip; prepare a *schedule of* his *appointments;* list the *contents of* his *travel folder;* make arrangements for obtaining the *tickets;* attach a *recap sheet* to the outside of the travel folder, as shown in Figure 16-10.

The underscored words create a certain amount of paperwork; and these paper items will be what he takes with him.

Preliminary Preparations. Your boss may travel by car, plane, train, or a combination of the modes of transportation.

If he plans to drive, see to it that he has a road map. If the city is strange to him, the following information, provided by the Local Chamber of Commerce Department of the National Chamber, may be of significant help to your office:

> Many local chambers of commerce prepare or have available a map of the city or area served. In some cases there is a small fee, but in many cases the maps are free. Lists of member hotel and motel facilities are also usually available. A visit to the chamber of commerce in any city is recommended.

Before you request reservations, you may want to ask some of the following questions, if your boss has not given you the necessary information that will enable you to make definite plans.

1. Will he be the only person for whom you must request travel and hotel or motel reservations?

2. Is the travel schedule to be worked out around his appointments? If so, find out how many appointments he has scheduled, the hour of each one, the place, and the purpose. If appointments must be arranged to coincide with his travel schedule, you must advise his appointments of his arrival date and time, as soon as the travel schedule is confirmed. (Any changes in a travel schedule must be relayed to the individuals who are scheduled to meet with your boss, if the changes affect any previously scheduled meetings.)

3. What time of day does he prefer to travel? Is he willing to get out of bed at the wee hours of the morning, or does he enjoy traveling in mid day?

4. If part of his trip must be made by car and you are responsible for requesting a car rental, find out what make and model he prefers to drive.

5. Is the payment of tickets handled through an account, or is it to be a cash transaction? Are the tickets to be delivered, mailed, or picked up?

6. Does he have air travel cards and other credit cards? If so, find out what the expiration dates are. (Incorporate this information and the card numbers in his personal section of the procedures manual discussed in another section of this book.)

When you have the above information, begin working out the details of his itinerary.

Use a form, for your rough draft of the itinerary, similar to Figure 16-1 while you are gathering travel details prior to confirmation.

Special reminders are typed at the bottom of the form; but the special reminders will not appear on the final draft of the itinerary in the arrangement shown on the form.

The form was originally designed for air travel, but the captions can be changed to agree with terminology of the other modes of transportation.

ITINERARY FOR (NAME OF PERSON)

Day and Date			Air Carrier and Flight	Airport
	Lv.	_____ : _____ (Time Zone)		
	Ar.	_____ : _____		
	Lv.	_____ : _____		
	Ar.	_____ : _____		
	Lv.	_____ : _____		
	Ar.	_____ : _____		
	Lv.	_____ : _____		
	Ar.	_____ : _____		

FARE: _____

CLASS OF SERVICE: _____

GROUND TRANSPORTATION: _____

SPECIAL INSTRUCTIONS FOR BAGGAGE: _____

FOOD SERVICE _____

TICKETS: Deliver _____ ; Mail _____ ; Pick up _____

CONFIRMED BY: _____

Figure 16-1. Itinerary Worksheet.

217

After travel arrangements have been made and the reservations confirmed, an itinerary in final form will resemble the sample in Figure 16-2. Type an original and at least two carbon copies of the itinerary—the original for your boss, one copy for the files, and a carbon copy for any family member or designated company official.

You may telephone or personally visit the carrier's office or request the services of a travel agency. Ask your boss what procedure he prefers.

If you don't know the name of the individual with whom you are working out the travel arrangements, ask for it. Work out the travel arrangements from beginning to end with the same individual whenever possible.

Travel by Plane.   The travel agent or ticket office personnel will be able to process your request efficiently if you tell the clerk exactly what your boss' schedule requires and what he wants in the way of service.

Before you contact any clerk, give some thought to the following questions:

1. What time of day must your boss arrive at his destination? (Consider the time it takes him to collect his baggage and travel from the airport to the meeting place.)

2. Does he prefer a particular class of service—coach, or jet first class, or any available service?

3. Does he prefer one carrier over others for specific trips?

4. Are you to consider economy first, or is time always to be considered more important than fare?

Ask for an alternate flight, just in case the first requested flight cannot be confirmed.

Ask for the check-in time prior to the scheduled departure. (Encourage your boss to be at the terminal at the specified time.)

Tell the reservations clerk what date the tickets must be in your office. (The type of transaction—cash or on account—may determine the procedure for obtaining the tickets. Check with your boss to find out what type of transaction it will be.)

Leave the telephone numbers of your office and your boss' home with the reservations clerk, so that you or your boss can be notified of any changes, should there be any.

ITINERARY FOR PAUL J. ADAMSON

(Kansas City: Albuquerque, Omaha, Kansas City)

Day and Date	Destination	Time	Carrier and Flight	Airport
Monday 10-3-	LV. KANSAS CITY, MISSOURI	8:10 a.m.	Frontier Airlines #711	Municipal
	Ar. Denver, Colorado	8:28 a.m.		Stapleton
	LV. DENVER, COLORADO	10:15 a.m.	Frontier Airlines #591	Stapleton
	Ar. Albuquerque, New Mexico	11:48 a.m.		Municipal
Wednesday 10-5-	LV. ALBUQUERQUE, NEW MEXICO	8:45 a.m.	Frontier Airlines #580	Municipal
	Ar. Denver, Colorado	10:00 a.m.		Stapleton
	LV. DENVER, COLORADO	11:50 a.m.	Frontier Airlines #566	Stapleton
	Ar. Omaha, Nebraska	3:42 p.m.		Eppley
Thursday 10-6-	LV. OMAHA, NEBRASKA	4:30 p.m.	Frontier Airlines #741	Eppley
	Ar. Kansas City, Missouri	5:02 p.m.		Municipal

Courtesy of Frontier Airlines, Denver, Colorado.

Figure 16-2. Itinerary for Travel by Plane.

When the tickets reach your office, compare your itinerary with the tickets. Check the date, departure time, and carrier and flight to be sure that the information typed on the itinerary corresponds with the completed passenger ticket. Be sure the ticket indicates a confirmed seat, if you requested it. See Figure 16-3.

Before your boss leaves the office, remind him of the check-in time, and remind him to re-confirm his confirmed ticket in each city from which he is scheduled to depart. (You might type the telephone numbers of the reservations offices in each city and attach this list to his itinerary.)

Travel by Train.   Be specific when requesting travel accommodations, whether you contact the railway ticket office or a travel agency. If you don't have a selection of brochures and other printed material, available to passengers, visit the ticket offices or travel agency; you will become more familiar with the services available on the routes your boss travels. Check with the source from which you obtain printed material to be sure that your information is current.

Prior to requesting train reservations, your preliminary preparations may necessitate another question-and-answer session.

1. What hour must your boss arrive in a particular city?

2. What type of accommodation does he prefer—first class, entitling him to Pullman facilities, or coach?

3. Will he want a round trip ticket or one way ticket?

4. Are you to request a car rental for him at his destination?

5. How will he want his baggage handled? If it is to be checked, how many pieces will he have?

Some of the things you will want to know when you contact the reservations clerk are:

1. The train number, name, and car number; departure and arrival schedules and the time zone.

2. The name of the station on arrival and the station of departure.

3. The dining facilities available. (Is dining car service available at all times or only during mealtimes?)

4. The other services available such as steward, stewardess, porter, coach attendant, and so on.

5. The check-in time for whatever accommodations are requested.

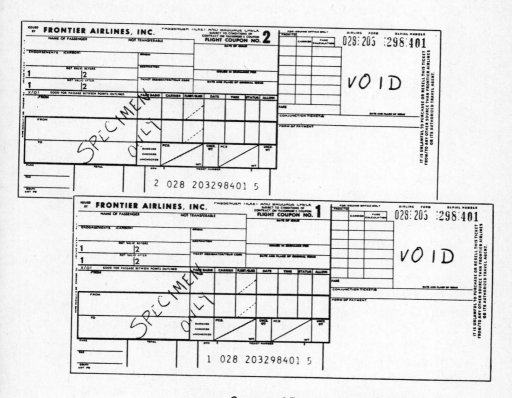

Courtesy of Frontier Airlines, Denver, Colorado.

Figure 16-3. Air Passenger Ticket.

6. The fare for the accommodations requested.

7. The credit cards, if any, that will be honored.

8. The date tickets must be picked up, if the tickets are not delivered to your office or mailed to your office.

When the tickets reach your office, check the accommodations reserved for your boss with those you have typed on the itinerary. (If you don't understand the code on the ticket, ask the reservations clerk to explain it to you.) Your boss may ask you what the symbols represent.

Type an original and at least two carbons copies of the itinerary. The original is sent along with your boss; one carbon copy is for the file. He may want his family to have a carbon copy, so the remaining copy would go to them.

NOTE: If your boss is on a special diet, he should make this known to the steward.

An illustration of an itinerary for a trip by train (Figure 16-4) is shown.

Passenger Cancellations.   It may be necessary to cancel travel plans. If so, notify the travel agent or ticket office immediately. A telephone call will enable the carrier to make the necessary space adjustments.

Unused Tickets.   Refund requests and credit for unused tickets should be submitted to the ticket agent or possibly the carrier's accounting office. The address of the carrier's accounting office may appear on the timetable.

Hotel Reservations.   Telephone, or write if time permits, for overnight accommodations at the hotel or motel specified by your boss. Give the reservations desk attendant the following information: Your boss' name, the mailing address of your office, the type of accommodations he wants, the date and time of arrival, and the date of departure.

If you telephone for reservations, *spell* your boss' name for the reservations desk attendant—willingly.

You may not be able to give the reservations desk attendant an exact arrival time. When this is the situation, ask that the accommodations be held for late arrival, and request that this notation be made on the confirmed reservation form.

Ask for the check-out time, and also ask the hotel or motel reservations desk attendant to mail you a written confirmation of the accommodations. When the confirmation is received in your office, make a note of the details that appear on the confirmation for your information while your boss is away. If the check-out time does not appear on the confirmation, write it on the form. (In your original communication with the reservations desk attendant, ask for the check-out time. Make a note of this and then check the confirmation form for printed details.) Place the written confirmation form or letter in your boss' travel folder.

```
                    ITINERARY FOR PAUL J. ADAMSON

                              November 10-20


TRAIN:  CITY OF SAN FRANCISCO          Pullman 1010, Roomette 8


Sunday    Lv. Omaha, Nebr.    2:55 AM (CT) UnPacRR(Union Station)
Sunday    Ar. Ogden, Utah     7:30 PM (MT) UnPacRR
Sunday    Lv. Ogden, Utah     8:30 PM (MT) SoPacRR
Monday    Ar. San Francisco   1:50 PM (PT) SoPacRR (*)
(*) Passengers use motor bus via Bay Bridge between Oakland
    (16th Street Station) and San Francisco (3rd Street).

RETURN TRIP

Sunday    Lv. San Francisco   2:15 PM (PT) SoPacRR (3rd St. Bus Stn)
Tuesday   Ar. Omaha           3:10 AM (CT) UnPacRR (Union Station)
```

Courtesy of Union Pacific Railroad Company, Omaha, Nebraska.

Figure 16-4. Itinerary for Travel by Train.

Learn the individual's name with whom the arrangements for overnight accommodations are being made. Follow-up information regarding the accommodations may then be directed to the individual who handled the original request. (For future reference, write the name, address, and telephone number of the hotel or motel in your procedures manual.)

Samples of confirmation forms appear in Figures 16-5 and 16-6.

Hotel Cancellations. Remain in the good graces of all those involved in your trip by notifying the hotel or motel reservations office of any cancellations. A telephone call from you to the people who attempted to make your trip comfortable may allow them to accommodate a traveler whose trip is as much a "last minute" thing as your cause of cancellation.

The Travel Folder. Prepare a summary form to be attached to the outside of the folder which your boss will take along on his trip. Information that will be typed on the summary form will be obtained from the correspondence that flows in and out of your office. The summary form is used for scheduled meetings, conventions, speaking engagements, or appointments.

When several meetings and appointments are scheduled out of town, he may be out of the office for several weeks. Label a separate folder for each meeting or speaking engagement.

An illustration of the summary form appears in Figure 16-7.

Before your boss leaves on his trip and if your office is equipped with a copying machine, reproduce the original correspondence. Keep the original correspondence for the office files and place the reproductions in the travel folder.

The travel folder should contain only *original* papers which your boss must present as his key to *admittance to special functions; hotel or motel reservations;* the *itinerary* and, of course, the *tickets.* Other original material may include such papers as the *list of his appointments* and a *list of the contents* of the travel folder.

All other papers in the travel folder should be copies. Weeks may pass before he returns to the office or before he has time to go through the travel folder after he does return to the office; but with the original correspondence in your office, you won't have to worry about incomplete files.

Type, in duplicate, the list of appointments which are scheduled throughout your boss' trip. Add to this list any addresses and telephone numbers of people he plans to contact while he is in another city. Also list unconfirmed appointments and visits; i.e., if the executive has invited certain individuals to contact him at

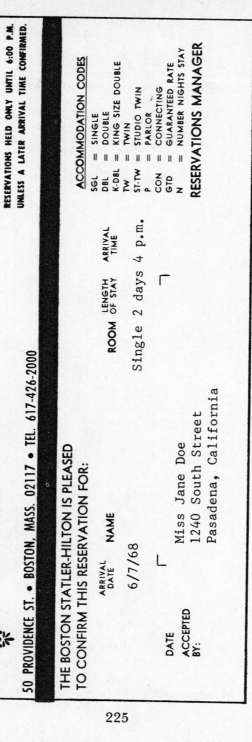

Figure 16-5. Guest Confirmation (Hotel).

Courtesy of The Boston Statler-Hilton, Boston, Massachusetts.

KAYCO   0-7-24982

CONFIRMATION OF RESERVATION

ACCOMMODATIONS ARE HELD ONLY UNTIL 6:00 P.M.
UNLESS SECURED BY GUARANTEE OR DEPOSIT.

Re:

ARRIVAL DATE	
DEPARTURE	

Lernando Courtright's
Beverly Wilshire Hotel

9500 Wilshire Boulevard
Beverly Hills, California 90213

ARRIVAL DATE	ARRIVAL TIME	DEPART. DATE	TYPE OF ACCOMMODATIONS	APPROX. RATE	GUARANTEED

REMARKS

THANK YOU FOR REQUESTING RESERVATIONS AT THE BEVERLY WILSHIRE HOTEL. IT IS NOT ALWAYS POSSIBLE TO HAVE ROOMS AVAILABLE FOR EARLY ARRIVAL, UNLESS REGISTERED IN THE PREVIOUS NIGHT. OUR CHECK OUT HOUR IS 2:00 P.M.

WE CONSIDER IT A PRIVILEGE TO INCLUDE YOU AMONG THE MANY DISTINGUISHED PERSONS WHO SELECT THE BEVERLY WILSHIRE HOTEL FOR THEIR LOS ANGELES ADDRESS.

_____   _____
        DATE   CONFIRMED BY

AIRPORT LIMOUSINE - DIRECT TO AND FROM INTERNATIONAL AIRPORT.

PRIVATE CAREY-CADILLAC LIMOUSINE - AVAILABLE ON REQUEST, TO OR FROM INTERNATIONAL AIRPORT.

TWX (213) 273-4397   TEL. (213) 275-4282

Courtesy of Beverly Wilshire Hotel, Beverly Hills, California.

Figure 16-6. Confirmation of Reservation (Hotel).

Sample reservation confirmation form. . .used when we do not send our usual personal letter of confirmation.*

_____

*Cited in a letter dated June 12, 1968 addressed to the writer.

MEETING/SPEAKING ENGAGEMENT

Date: _____ (_____)
                              Day
Time: _____ A. M. or P. M.

Place: _____

City and State: _____, _____

    Tel. No.: _____

Purpose of Meeting: _____

_____

_____

Guest Speaker: _____

Special Material Needed: _____

_____

Reservations

    Travel: _____
        Check-In Time: _____

    Hotel: _____
        Check-Out Time: _____

CHECK THE HOUR, IF IN DIFFERENT TIME ZONE.

tks
rev. 6/68

Figure 16-7. Meeting/Speaking Engagement Summary Form.

CONFIRMED APPOINTMENTS

Day, Date and Hour	City	Name/Address	Purpose of Meeting
Monday, 10-3- One o'clock	Albuquerque, N.M.*	John Arthur (realtor) 701 Porters Avenue (505) CU1-2000	Discuss acreage development
Wednesday, 10-5- Ten o'clock	Omaha, Nebraska	Everett Payne 543 Orchard (402) 435-6862	Dedication ceremony
1:30 P. M.	Omaha, Nebraska	Jack D. Dudley Vice President First Loan Company Trescott and Main (402) 216-1533	Panel discussion on economic forecast

* Tuesday, 10-4- After 8:30 A. M. - Clifton Marshall, 24, master's degree plus two years' experience; interview for public relations position. (Copy of his letter dated September 23 requesting personal interview enclosed. Your reply dated September 28 invited Mr. Marshall to telephone you at hotel [after 8:30 A. M.] to arrange for interview.)

Figure 16-8. List of Appointments for Trip.

ITINERARY
Denver-Salt Lake City-San Francisco-Denver
Joseph Smith

DAY	DATE	TIME	CITY	VIA
Monday	March 11	Leave 8:55 p.m. Arrive 9:59 p.m.	Denver to Salt Lake City	UAL Flt. #177
			Reservations at Holiday Inn - Airport 1659 W. North Temple Salt Lake City, Utah 84116 Phone: 801-322-1045	
Tuesday	March 12	9:00 a.m.	CAB Prehearing Conference	
		7:00 p.m.	Dinner with John Doe Four Seasons Restaurant	
Wednesday	March 13	9:00 a.m.	CAB Prehearing Conference	
		leave 6:40 p.m. arrive 7:10 p.m.	Salt Lake City to San Francisco	UAL Flt. #367
			Reservations at Hotel Mark Hopkins Nob Hill San Francisco, Calif. 94106 Phone: 415-392-3434	
Thursday	March 14	8:30 a.m.	Symposium on Air Safety	
		1:00 p.m.	Luncheon with Fred Hall Fairmont Hotel	
Friday	March 15	8:30 a.m.	Symposium on Air Safety	
		leave 5:15 p.m. arrive 8:30 p.m.	San Francisco to Denver	UAL Flt. #344

Courtesy of United Air Lines, Chicago, Illinois

Figure 16-9. Itinerary Including Accommodations and Appointments.

his hotel or motel while he is in a particular city, indicate this on the list. Briefly describe how the invitation was extended and the reason for the call.

Figure 16-8 is a sample of a list of appointments.

If you type the summary form which is attached to the outside of the travel folder, in duplicate, it may not be necessary to type both the summary and the list of confirmed appointments. The procedure that is most helpful to your boss is the one you would use.

Your boss may prefer to have his travel arrangements, hotel accommodations, and scheduled commitments all on the same sheet. A sample of this method is shown in Figure 16-9.

To the inside front of the travel folder, attach a list of the papers and items included for each appointment. It might be helpful to number each item in the folder to correspond with the number on the list of contents.

The list of contents in any one folder may resemble Figure 16-10.

LIST OF CONTENTS

City: Albuquerque, New Mexico

1. Carbon copy of itinerary (Original is with tickets. This is extra copy.)
2. Copy of letter dated March 7 from John Arthur—outlines proposals in connection with acreage development.
3. Copy of Eric Harris' itinerary. (Mr. Harris is attorney who will also attend meeting.)
4. Confirmation of reservations: Hotel Parker-East.

Figure 16-10. Folder Contents Sheet.

The amount of paperwork your boss does "on the road" will determine what supplies you pack for his briefcase. However, every folder should contain an executive-type pad, pencils, and pens.

Your boss, as a traveler, acts as an ambassador of the company he represents. In addition to the pertinent papers and the primary purpose of his business trip, you can: (1) help him promote good will for the company; (2) help him interest a potential customer in the company's products; (3) help him promote a worthy cause even though it is unrelated to the purpose of the trip.

What He Takes with Him. Without overloading his brief-case, include among his "must-take" papers a *publicity packet*. The publicity packet might consist of brochures which briefly tell the story of the company, or some introductory material. You might also include a recap of organizational activities involving company personnel. It may also be worthwhile to include a list of community projects which the company sponsors, as a public relations gesture.

The publicity packet may be prepared or assembled in advance of any business trip. Material which is not pertinent to the trip and which your boss definitely does not want to take with him may be removed prior to his departure.

The travel folders should be arranged according to the cities visited, the date, and the hour of the appointment.

What He Brings Back. When your boss returns to the city, the travel folders should be returned to the office for clearing.

File the papers which have been removed from the office for the trip, if there are any; dispose of any copies of correspondence according to office policy; write thank-you letters to individuals who entertained your boss and to firms and persons who were especially helpful to him during his trip.

The Travel Expense Report. If your boss is out of town for any length of time, he will have recorded his travel expenses during the trip. A travel expense form should be placed in the travel folders, even though your boss may not complete the form until he returns to the office.

You may be expected to complete the travel expense form. Gather all the receipts, complete the form, and attach the receipts to the duplicate copy[1] of the travel expense form. Submit the completed form for your boss' signature, and promptly submit the signed form to the proper department for processing.

An illustration of an Expense Report (furnished through the courtesy of Wilson Jones Company) is shown in Figure 16-11.

---

[1] This procedure will vary with the location of the accounting office, etc.

EXPENSE REPORT

PERIOD ENDING _____ 19___

CITY AND STATE	LODGING	TRANSPORTATION		AUTOMOBILE EXPENSES			MEALS	LOCAL TAXI & CARFARE	OTHER EXPENSES		DAILY TOTAL
		AIR, RAIL ETC.	LIMOUSINE TAXI ETC.	MILEAGE	DESCRIPTION	AMOUNT			ITEMIZE	AMOUNT	
S U N D A Y											
M O N D A Y											
T U E S D A Y											
W E D N E S D A Y											
T H U R S D A Y											
F R I D A Y											
S A T U R D A Y											

TOTALS

EXPLANATION OF OTHER EXPENSES

☐ DEDUCT FROM MY ADVANCE

☐ MAIL CHECK TO

SIGNATURE

APPROVED BY

TOTAL EXPENSES

Grayline "SNAP-A-WAY" FORM 44-950 2-PARTS

Courtesy of Wilson Jones Company, Chicago, Illinois.

Figure 16-11 Expense Report (Front)

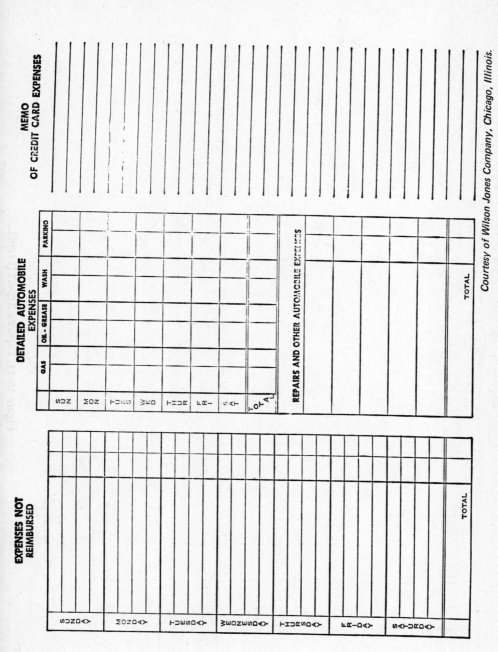

Courtesy of Wilson Jones Company, Chicago, Illinois.

Figure 16-11. Expense Report (Back).

233

17

A Few Special Duties

A branch office generally obtains most of the necessary stationery and supplies from the home office or a regional office. Requisition forms would be supplied to the branch offices.

When stationery and supplies are needed by the branch office, the requisition form is completed and mailed to the designated office. Certain days of the month may be stipulated as ordering dates, and it may be company policy that stationery and supply requests be sufficient to last the office at least two or three months. Which date is designated as your supply-ordering date? What is the suggested quantity of supplies to be ordered for your office use? Who is authorized to sign the supply order form?

Ordering Stationery and Supplies.   Type the supply order form in duplicate. Retain a copy in your "Pending" file until all of the supplies that you ordered are received. Check the supplies ordered and those shipped to your office to be sure that you received the identical items and the quantities requested. Place a check mark and write the date on the copy of the order form to show that the supplies were received. When all supplies ordered have been received by your office, file your copy in the appropriate file. At various intervals, your office may be required to submit figures for office expense reports. A carbon copy may be your record for accounting purposes.

The Supply Room.   A smaller business may have a supply room in the building and every employee is free to help himself to whatever supplies are needed, and no written request is required. If you have access to any and all supplies, it is still wise to record the supplies you use in your office. Design a simple form, use it whenever you replenish your supplies for the office, and file the form for future reference.

There may come a time when management decides a requisition form is to be completed before supplies can be obtained, or that the stationery and supplies expense is not to exceed a stipulated amount. You would be able to estimate your office needs by studying your filed copy of the form.

If you list the supplies you need before you go to the supply room, you won't have to try to remember each item; you can save yourself a second trip to the supply room.

Recognize the importance of keeping records, even if an item seems relatively small. It may inaugurate an inventory system for supplies put some control on the supplies used, particularly when everyone has the "key" to the supply room.

Special-Order Supplies. Holiday stationery and supplies may have to be special ordered. Find out what the company policy is concerning special-occasion stationery.

A Stationery and Supply Record form might be designed something like Figure 17-1.

WHAT TO DO WITH LEISURE TIME

After all the mail has been taken care of and the boss is out of town, some of the following suggestions may help you fill the void office hours if you are faced with leisure time.

Prepare for Rush Correspondence and Mailing Lists in Advance. Do as much work in advance as is feasible and beneficial, timewise. Avoid doing too much work ahead of time; do the work that is least likely to have major changes. Address a supply of envelopes to individuals who are to receive reports and copies of correspondence frequently. Type envelopes during your spare time for mailing lists your company has. Keep an extra pack of addressed envelopes on hand for that rush press release. Doublecheck the addresses before the actual mailing date to make sure that no names have been added to the list and that no address has been changed. New envelopes must be typed for mailing list additions and corrections.

STATIONERY AND SUPPLY RECORD
for
Trust Department

Date	Qty.	Item No. or (Indicate if special-order item) Description	Price	Total

Figure 17-1. Stationery and Supply Record Form.

Design Forms for Duplication, if a Form Saves Time.   Routine work may be simplified by preparing a form on which only the dollar amounts or comparison figures change from time to time. Routine duties need not imply that the same assignment is performed every day at the same time, although this does happen depending on the nature of the business and what your assignments are. So, the frequency of a specific task performed by someone in your office or you alone will determine the convenience of using a form.

Whenever it is practical, prepare a form which can be easily duplicated or mimeographed. Many times, by using a form, in addition to saving time, you can prevent overlooking important details. In any office, details are vital to the smooth operation of the business.

Clean Your Office.   Take good care of the equipment provided for your use, to get the maximum efficiency from your mechanical helpers. Follow the directions outlined in booklets supplied with the equipment in your office.

Change the typewriter ribbon when necessary, and clean the typewriter keys for good clear copies.

Wipe away dust, and mop up any spills.

Use a stiff brush to clean the date stamps. Residue collects in the cutouts on the rubber stamps. Clean these for neat impressions.

Describe Your Secretarial Duties in a Procedures Manual.   A detailed description of the duties you perform will be invaluable when your work must be performed by someone else. Should it be necessary to call in a substitute secretary she would be able to take care of your boss and the work flow much more efficiently if a guide is available. During vacation periods or sick leave, the procedures manual will enable the substitute to perform the work the same way you do the work. A procedures manual will eliminate a barrage of questions directed to your boss—questions such as, "How is this to be completed?" or "Where do I send the copies?"

In addition to the detailed descriptions of your duties, the procedures manual should include samples of forms used and samples of documents in completed form; a glossary of the business terminology; a floorplan of the building.

CORPORATE STRUCTURE

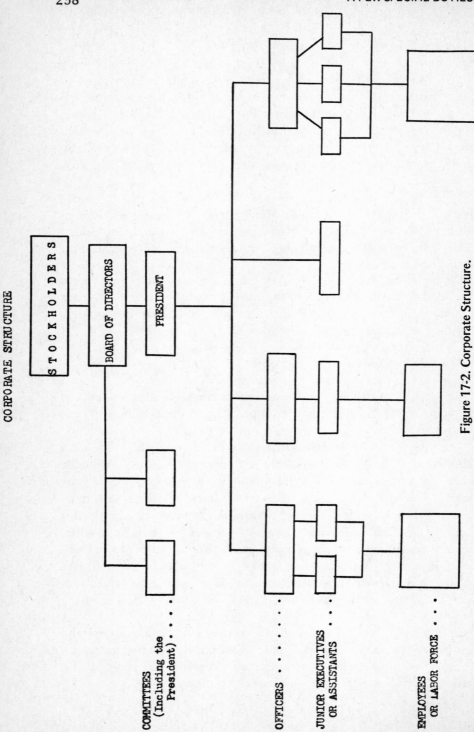

Figure 17-2. Corporate Structure.

STOCKHOLDERS

BOARD OF DIRECTORS

PRESIDENT

COMMITTEES
(Including the
President) · · · · ·

OFFICERS · · · · · ·

JUNIOR EXECUTIVES
OR ASSISTANTS · · · ·

EMPLOYES
OR LABOR FORCE · · ·

Management deserves a helping hand. By outlining the office procedures, a secretary can help soften the jolt many offices experience during employee "turnover" sessions.

Prepare the Organization Chart. The complete layout of the company distribution of duties in chart form could be a time-consuming project. You probably would not begin such a project on your own initiative until employment with the company reached a total of several months. Before you begin such a task, ask your boss if time spent referring to it makes the preparation time worthwhile. He may feel there would be no need for the chart.

However, if you are instructed to prepare an organization chart, stalling for time is out of the question. Perhaps the information and a rough sketch will be given to you to simply recopy. Or you may have to spend some time searching for the information.

The size and detail will depend on the purpose for which the chart will be used.

Figure 17-2 briefly depicts corporate structure.

Some of the authority boxes could be permanently labeled with the traditional business titles. As the chart develops "legs," pencil in the titles and names of those in charge. This will allow for promotional and replacement changes without having to reconstruct the entire durable chart.

18

Personal Services for Your Boss

Added to your other responsibilities will be the special services you perform to assist your boss in keeping his desk in neat order. These duties will probably be only the "light housekeeping" chores.

As a convenience to your boss, when you arrive at the office, prepare his office and his desk for the day. The following chores are not assigned to "doting" secretaries; they are assigned as a convenience and time-saver for a busy boss.

1. Switch on the light.

2. Keep a clean cloth handy so that you may dust the desk (just in case he left the office late and after the janitor finished the nightly cleaning).

3. Empty the ashes from the ashtrays into a paper towel. Instead of dumping the ashes directly into the wastebasket, use a paper towel. Then wipe the ashtray with a damp paper towel.

4. Wipe the mouthpiece of telephones frequently—with a *clean* cloth.

5. Fill the water Thermos and wash the drinking glasses.

6. Sharpen pencils and fill the fountain pens. Wash the pens and pen holders regularly to keep them in good working condition.

7. Check ballpoint pens to make sure they write smoothly. Replace cartridges; if necessary, replace the entire writing instrument.

8. Turn the calendar, and list his daily appointments. Save all calendar notations until you know he has taken care of any notes

or instructions. Ask him about the notations before you throw away any notes he has written on the calendar or on any scratch pads.

9. See that the room temperature is comfortable for him. Check with maintenance personnel, if it isn't, so that his office will be comfortable when he arrives for work.

10. Change date stamps and wall calendars.

11. Keep him supplied with matches, if he smokes.

12. Replenish the various desk items such as rubber bands, map pins, staples, paper clips, desk pads, calling cards; and keep the stamp pads inked, if he has one or several.

At the end of the day, be sure that his office lights are switched off and that the office door is locked.

Your own desk, of course, will be as well supplied for your own convenience and efficiency in performing the tasks assigned to you.

Know Where to Contact Your Boss.   For your "business" information only, know where you can contact him at all times during the regular work day. Very important telephone messages, unexpected but important visitors' messages, and other information which should be conveyed to him immediately make it imperative that you know where you can contact him.

Cancel His Dessert, if Necessary.   Find out where your boss eats lunch and where he usually takes his guests when he entertains during the lunch hour. Sometimes the conversation may go well into the time set aside for his first appointment following lunch. Your boss may not realize time is passing by.

If a scheduled visitor arrives and you suspect your boss is relaxing, go to another office, call the restaurant and talk with your boss. Tell him his appointment has arrived at the office. You might suggest that you give the visitor a tour of the newest addition to the building; this will occupy him until your boss can return to the office without showing embarrassment.

When you do take the visitor to your boss' office, a statement such as: "I was so anxious to show Mr. Lane the newest thing in buildings that I took the liberty to borrow some of the appointment time" may help blur the late schedule.

If your boss approved of the manner in which you handle

situations, he may tell you or he may not say a word about your methods. If he doesn't approve, no doubt he will tell you.

Take Note of Where Your Boss Prefers to Be.   If your boss slips out the back door without telling you that he is leaving, take heed! This action may indicate that he prefers mingling with the crowd instead of sitting at his desk or dictating letters.

Find out how much time your boss spends in the office. You can do this without asking. Look at the previous year's calendar. Notice how many meetings appear on the calendar and the days blocked off for out-of-town trips. This will give you a clue about his "office attendance." This may suggest that he prefers to farm out office details to other individuals—namely you.

Make a habit of gathering all the details necessary for answering the mail and returning telephone calls.

Emergency Telephone Numbers.   Make a list of the telephone numbers of the people who are important to your boss. The day may come when you must reach the barber, mechanic, fire department, police, dentist, physician, highway patrol, minister or priest, ambulance service, or hospital.

Begin Your Boss' Book of Memoirs.   The incoming mail and the outgoing mail will give you some idea of the amount of territory your boss covers. Find out what newspapers cover his life—business and social—and which newspapers are delivered to your office.

You will want this information and a pair of scissors in order to begin a "scrapbook" for your boss. Clip out the articles about the activities of his family, his own activities, professional achievements, and civic awards. Date the articles, and indicate from which newspaper or publication the article was clipped.

Compile His Biographical Sketch.   The book of memories will then be an aid in compiling your boss' biographical sketch, or in revising it whenever necessary.

Compose Social and Quasi-Personal Letters.   The activities of his business associates and social contacts will occasionally warrant drafting a note of thanks, congratulations, or a note of regret to an invitation to a social event. A death will be a time for an expression of sorrow.

Learn your boss' form of writing and have these notes ready (on his personal stationery) for his signature, particularly if he has been out of the office for a few days. Of course, he will appreciate them just as much if you were to have the notes ready for his signature when he returns from lunch.

You'll know what words to use when typing notes and letters for him by his verbal reaction to the various situations. The notes must be individual, not a form-letter type message. It need not be more than one sentence as long as it conveys a sincere feeling. Every boss has favorite words and phrases. The letter you write for his signature must "read" just like he "sounds."

Omit Reference Initials. Omit the reference initials on social and quasi-personal letters, but keep the records straight by re-inserting the carbon copy of the letter and typing your reference initials on the file copy only. The ink impression of the typewriter keys may be sufficient code to indicate that the reference initials appear only on the carbon copy, or you may want to circle the initials with a colored pencil.

The technique mentioned above to be used by secretaries who compose letters for the boss' signature, may also be used when the boss dictates a personal letter. Type the reference initials only on the carbon copy.

SAMPLE NOTES

Congratulations (Election Winner)

Dear Curtis:
    Two hundred seventy-five thousand people just can't be wrong. I'm proud to live in a state where we can depend on your leadership. Congratulations!
                                        Sincerely,

    NOTE: If he won by a wide margin of votes, the foregoing letter may be suitable. It might not be considered a compliment to mention numbers if the election had been won by a narrow margin.

Thank You (Gift)

Dear Harold:
    I know everyone here in the office would like to personally thank you for the delicious box of fruit.

Realizing it would be unfair to bury your desk at this busy time (those year-end reports keep increasing in size and number), here is a great big "thank you" from all of us.

Sincerely,

Dear Don:

Your gracious gift was a pleasant surprise and it is a compliment to our service that you remembered our twenty-fifth "business anniversary."

The wall maps are interesting, colorful, and the walnut frames match our office furniture.

Thank you very much.

Sincerely,

Award Recipient

Dear Wayne:

Last night when fellow citizens placed you on the business-world throne as the "Executive of the Year," I nearly lost my entire work force!

As a business associate, I know you are most deserving of this honor—heartiest congratulations, Wayne.

Sincerely,

Engagement

Dear Ann:

I read about your engagement in our daily paper yesterday. May I add my good wishes to your "Reservoir of Joy." With such natural charm, your happy engagement can lead only to much happiness in the future.

Sincerely,

Marriage

Dear Helen:

Distance prevented me from personally wishing you much joy as you and Bill begin your married life. My best wishes for your future happiness.

Sincerely,

Promotion (Relocation)

Dear George:
 Houston is gaining a special family. How proud I am
to say, "I know him very well." Good wishes always to
you, Carol, and the young men in your family.
                                        Sincerely,

Death

Dear Mrs. Allison:
 Only good thoughts cross my mind when I think of
your late husband. Many, many people will remember
his wonderful sense of humor and enthusiasm. It was a
privilege to be associated with him.
                                        Sincerely,

Compile His Business Associates Directory.   The business
associates directory will contain telephone numbers frequently
called and it should include the addresses of those firms and
individuals with which your boss frequently communicates.

In Chapter 3, "Office Telephone Calls," it was suggested that
the recorded telephone calls be filed. The business associates
directory is one reason for saving the recorded telephone calls.

Messages left by visitors can also be used in compiling the
business associates directory. (The file folder might be labeled
"Telephone and Visitor Messages.")

The mailing addresses of firms can be obtained for the directory
from dictated material in your shorthand pad and from the
letterhead of the various firms.

You may want to categorize the directory according to the type
of business with the names listed alphabetically. For instance, all
the insurance companies would be grouped together, then arranged alphabetically; all the banks would be grouped together,
the hotels, the associations in which the company holds membership; architects; contractors; and so on.

Compile His Social Directory.   You have probably worked for your boss long enough now to know who is in his social circle. From the letters he dictates, you can judge by the contents whether his visits are all-business or business and social.

Leaf through your shorthand pad and the telephone and visitors messages for addresses and telephone numbers, and begin arranging the material for your boss' social directory.

If your boss travels much of the time, it might be well to list the individuals' names and addresses geographically and also alphabetically.

Opposite the man's name, type the name of his wife and the names of the children, if known.

The social contact may stem from previous business transactions, so the business address may be the only address available. When you do learn the home address and telephone number, add this to the list and indicate which is the business address and telephone number and which is the home address and telephone number.

This social directory would be useful during the holiday season. Offer to address (in handwriting) Christmas cards and other greeting cards. (Your list should include members of his family with whom he keeps in contact primarily by mail if distance separates them.)

Type the Checks for His Personal Bills.   When your boss allows you to type the checks in payment of any bills, figure first any discounts applicable to the particular bill before writing the check.

On that portion of the bill that you are to retain for your boss' records, make a notation to show the date the bill was paid and the number of the check written for payment.

After all the checks have been typed, run an adding machine tape on the amounts due. Then run an adding machine tape on the amounts typed on each check. The two totaled lists should be the same.

On separate sheets of paper categorize the bills. One sheet may be for doctor and medical bills, another for clothes purchases, another for utilities, and so on. Head the sheets as in Figure 18-1.

File the sheets in the respective folders and place the portion of the bill kept for personal records in a pocket inside the folder. The total amount spent would be totaled at the end of the year, and

<u>(Name of Employer)</u>

DRUG BILLS PAID FROM PERSONAL ACCOUNT

<u>Date Paid</u>	<u>Payee</u>	<u>Amount</u>	<u>Total</u>
3-9	The Neighbor Drug Store	$ 20.00	
4-15	Coaster Drug	7.00	
7-21	Coaster Drug	2.00	
12-9	The Neighbor Drug Store	1.00	$30.00

Figure 18-1.

may be of some help when the income tax reports must be prepared.

Record His Personal Gifts to Others. Prepare a sheet of paper for recording donations and contributions to others. See the sample in Figure 18-2.

<u>PERSONAL CONTRIBUTIONS</u>

<u>Date</u>	Check <u>Number</u>	<u>Payee</u>	<u>Amount</u>	<u>Total</u>
1-2-63	1493	County Heart Fund	$20.00	

Figure 18-2.

Make a List of His Credit Cards. When a credit card is issued to your boss, list the credit card number, the date of expiration, and the name of the issuing company on a sheet of paper. The loss of any credit card should be reported to the issuing company. See the sample in Figure 18-3 for the headings.

CREDIT CARDS

Date of Issue	Date of Expiration	Name of Issuing Company	Card Number
9-1-65	10-31-66	Circle-Globe	84 391 00

Figure 18-3.

Record His Insurance Policies.   Prepare a sheet for recording the various insurance policies, including group insurance, if your boss has this type of coverage. As the premium notices are received and paid, record the coverage period, the date the premium was paid, the amount paid, and the number of the check written in payment of the policy premium. Figure 18-4 is a sample.

Handling Your Boss' Money.   Your boss may instruct you to deposit his payroll check when he is out of the office. Or, handling his check may be one of your regular responsibilities. Call the bank and ask for the exact procedure you should follow when you are to deposit his checks.

If the checks are not endorsed, the bank may advise you to type special wording on the back of the checks; or you may be advised that upon presentment at the bank, the check without an endorsement will be stamped with a special stamp by the bank's employee.

When you are instructed to deposit your boss' checks, prepare the deposit ticket in duplicate, and retain the duplicate for his records. Figure 18-5 is a sample of a personalized deposit ticket.

Ask the bank institution about banking services by mail. Perhaps this would be a convenience to your office, particularly at a time when you are alone in the office and cannot leave it

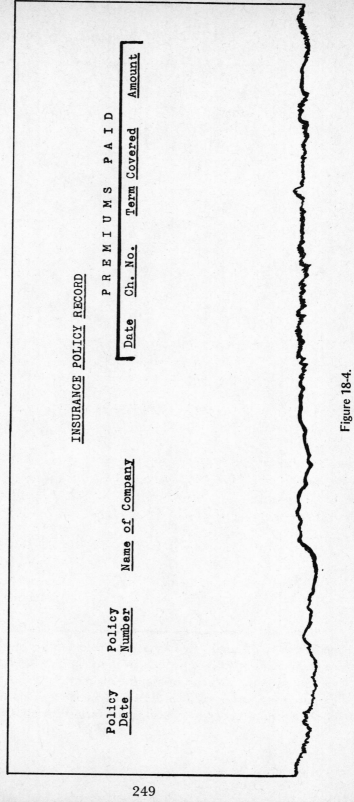

Figure 18-4.

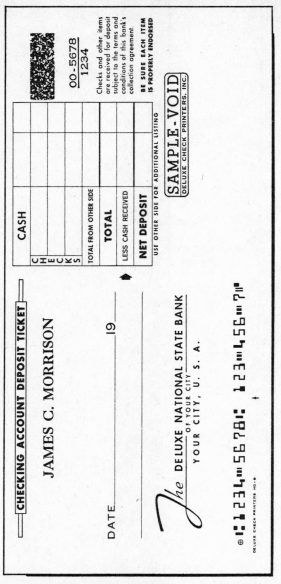

Courtesy of First National Bank of Kansas City, Kansas City, Missouri.

Figure 18-5. Personalized Deposit Ticket.

unattended. It might just be a preferred method for any number of reasons. It would be worth an inquiry, but follow the method your boss prefers when you handle his money.

Sometime you may be told to exchange a check for cash. The check cashing procedure, also, may vary with banks. Call or visit the banking institution to learn what requirements must be met before the bank will honor checks presented in this manner.

Annual Reminders.   The first part of October may not be too soon to remind your boss to consider ordering *holiday cards and stationery.*

To retain the truly personal touch, ask him to sign a few cards each week. After the cards have been signed and addressed, affix postage stamps instead of using the office postage meter. The holiday wishes from your boss will be personal wishes.

Remind your boss to write for *vacation literature* early.

Remind your boss to vote on *election days;* if he won't be in the city, remind him of the absentee ballot.

Mini Notes.   Your boss may be invited to any number of meetings and special events year after year. When the depth of his involvement is only that he "plans to attend," type pertinent information on a slip of paper small enough for him to tuck into his pocket. Your boss can then refer to the note for the names of the special people and guest speakers. (Figure 18-6.)

```
              Father and Son Banquet

    Date:  July 10, 19--      Time:  7:30 p.m.

    Place:  High school cafeteria

    High School Principal:  Paul Stuart

    Toastmaster:  Gerald Trolley

    Special Guest:  Harris Nevin (Exchange student)

    Cost:  $2.75 per plate--pick up tickets at the
       door
```

Figure 18-6.

Special Interests.   Call your boss' attention to meetings open to the public if they pertain to anything that might interest him.

19

Office Manners, Dress, and Etiquette

You must want to say the right thing and make the proper gesture before you radiate an aura of confidence and control of your secretarial position.

Set an Example for Co-workers. Co-workers are not to become sounding boards for personal or business annoyances. Assumptions and personal friction are not to be used as foundations for gossip. Don't try to buy office pals with "little treats" in exchange for friendship.

Employment tenure does not put you at liberty to ask personal questions of newcomers or anyone else, nor should you make statements in an attempt to pull a personal tale from a co-worker. Questions that pry into one's privacy are unpardonable. Concentrate on your responsibilities and try to improve your working knowledge.

Coffee Break Conduct. Coffee breaks: A period of time to regenerate for the rest of the workday. Break time begins when you leave your desk, not when you arrive at the coffee shop or reach the coffee room. Break time includes "travel time."

Never discuss people or mention names during coffee breaks; some one person may thrive on passing along anecdotes, simply for the sake of chattering. Don't give anyone the slightest chance to distort your circle of associates.

Pick Up After Yourself. Make sure you discard paper cups you have used; empty the ashtray you use, if you smoke.

Lipstick-smudged cigarette ends and stained cups are no treat for anyone else to discard.

Throw used paper towels and tissues in the waste basket. A used tissue, even if it is a pastel color, does not add to the color scheme of any office. Never leave tissues on your desk, at the postage meter, or in the lounge. It isn't sanitary to transport used tissues from your hand to the typewriter, to the desk, and on to the paper cutter.

Use the ashtrays for ashes, not as receptacles for rubber bands, paper clips, scraps of paper, or candy and gum wrappers.

Children in the Office. Baby-sitters should not be invited to walk the children to the office for show-and-tell sessions. A working mother should not allow the children to remain with her for the "rest of the afternoon." Make arrangements to have reliable baby-sitters look after the children at home. They should understand your obligation to your employer during office hours.

Friends and Relatives Telephoning the Office. Friends and relatives should not be encouraged to telephone or visit you at the office. Emergency calls, of course, do not come under the general "personal" category. Although many employers permit personal calls, the number and length of the conversation time should be limited.

How to Embarrass an Entire Office Staff. If you want to embarrass the entire office staff, cling to a personal call. When you receive such a call and a typing assignment simultaneously, clamp the telephone receiver between your ear and your shoulder, and continue talking while you attempt to type the brief note or not-so-brief assignment. When you finish typing the assignment, place the telephone receiver on your desk, since you have not concluded the telephone conversation. Rush the typed item to whomever presented it to you; walk hurriedly back to your desk, pick up the telephone arm and continue the conversation.

NOTE: This could be habit-forming if not curtailed, and it is not recommended for anyone.

You and Your Supervisor. When you know that a business transaction is dangling and the lunch hour is approaching, offer to either postpone your lunch hour or to change your lunch hour with another secretary, if lunch hours are staggered. If this is not necessary, cut the lunch hour short so that your supervisor can count on your return to the office within minutes.

If your supervisor is waiting for an important telephone call and refuses to leave the office during his lunch time, offer to pick up a sandwich and something to drink for him.

Gift-Giving.   Never put your supervisor in the embarrassing "Here's yours. Where's mine?" situation at Christmas time or any other time. Most employers do not expect gifts from employees, although it is not unusual for an employer to entertain at traditional get-togethers and distribute individual gifts. In some offices, all employees contribute money for the purchase of one item to be given to the manager or top official in the organization.

Company Get-Togethers.   Your consumption of alcoholic drinks should not go beyond the point where you lose control of being a well-mannered secretary. Better that your style of socializing with office personnel remain on the conservative side at company functions than for you to approach work the following day with the feeling that you could be a target for criticism by having been overly affectionate toward co-workers.

The Open Door Policy.   Respect your boss' time and position. He may have an open door policy, but don't wander into his office just because he does not have anyone sitting across the desk from him. What may appear to be free time is usually needed for important business decisions and concentration.

Time Off.   Asking for time off should be kept to a minimum. Illness and emergencies cannot be arranged ahead of time. Many companies consider a certain number of days as sick leave for each employee.

When circumstances are such that you must have time off from work, telephone your supervisor at the earliest reasonable hour so that he can arrange for temporary help or some assistance, if needed.

Announced, or surprise, visits from friends and relatives from out of town are not the best reasons for "needing" time off. Many companies grant employees vacations with pay. Make plans to entertain out-of-town visitors during your vacation.

One supervisor rearranged his Friday work schedule for three weeks in a row because the secretary requested and was granted time off to entertain a relative the first Friday; she traveled to another town for an appointment the next Friday; and the following Friday she traveled in another direction to hear her husband's speech. She saved up two fifteen-minute coffee breaks each day for a week to make up for the time off. Two weeks later she was on her scheduled vacation.

Shaking Hands. Offer your hand to the businessman or office visitor when he is introduced to you only if his hand is free. For the man who has to shuffle portfolios, shaking hands can turn into a series of awkward motions.

Your Personal Care. Perhaps two minutes out of every hour in the office you are the feature to the office visitor, but sixty minutes out of every hour you may be one of many employees; therefore, you must not be mistaken for anyone other than a secretary for at least eight hours a day.

The day should begin with a bath, application of deodorant, an oral hygiene treatment, fresh makeup application, followed with a sprinkling of dusting powder, a splash of toilet water or cologne. During the day, freshen your breath with the breath sprays available or swish with clear water.

Brush your teeth after eating and use an effective mouthwash. A bottle of concentrated mouthwash takes up little room in a handbag.

Hair should be clean and arranged in a neat, manageable style.

Open perfume bottles after five.

Nail polish can be flattering to hands that are carefully manicured. Whether you wear colorless or tinted polish is a matter of personal taste, but the polish should be free of a chipped appearance.

Remove traces of makeup from your fingertips by lightly rubbing pumice over the fingertips. (If traces of creams and makeup are not removed from the fingertips, a fingerprint may stain the letterhead or decorate a piece of transparent tape which in turn shows up on the paper to which the tape has been attached.)

Apply a dollop of hand lotion each time you wash your hands.

The Appropriate Dress.   Clothes must be clean, pressed and they should fit properly. You will be comfortable knowing that you are dressed appropriately.

If you *think business* when you dress for work each day, you cannot be so far off that you will give an onlooker the impression that you intend to go partying any minute.

Sheer materials should not be selected for office attire. Ski jackets and ski clothes are primarily for the slopes. Culottes and sportswear should be purchased for sporting events, not for office wear.

This does not imply that a secretary must dress without style and in drab colors. A secretary can wear beautiful basic clothes—simple lines in neat and suitable fabrics, in a variety of colors.

Posture.   Good posture improves the appearance of one's clothes. Project an efficient and graceful "you": Stand with shoulders back and relaxed, head straight, stomach flat, buttocks tucked under, and relax the knees.

When seated, keep knees and feet together. Here is one foot placement that is comfortable: Cross ankles and pull your legs to the side of the chair from which your forward leg extends, i.e., cross the right ankle over your left ankle and pull your legs to the right-hand side of the chair. You can alternate positions by crossing your left ankle over your right ankle and pulling your legs to the left side of the chair.

A Scent Tip

Scents are often classified as floral, spicy, Oriental, etc. As a career woman for twelve months and all seasons, the scents could very well be classified as seasonal scents. Select fragrances for summer wear and other scents for wintertime wear. Below is a list of weather-weight favorites, favorites because the scent seems to blend with special colors.

Season and Fragrance	Color Association
Summer:	
Carnegie Pink Cologne	
Mist by Hattie Carnegie	
Perfumes	Pink

Fall:
    Golden Woods Cologne
    by Max Factor   Both of these fragrances
                          go well with the earth
    Twig Cologne Mist by   colors: tan, brown, green,
    Rexall   gold

Winter:
    Hypnotique Parfum
    Cologne by Max Factor   Summer-sky blue
                          woolens

Anytime:
    Cabochard Eau de
    Toilette by Grés   Especially compatible
                          with black or white.

    Youth Dew Cologne
    by Estée Lauder   All colors
    Royal Secret Luxury
    Cologne by Germaine
    Monteil   All colors

Of course, there are many other scent selections that would certainly be appropriate for daytime and anytime wear.

A Time to Travel.   Before you leave town, check your supplies—letterhead, carbon, pencils, stamps, envelopes, pens, and special documents or whatever you will need. Make arrangements ahead of time for renting a typewriter in the city where you will be working, or plan to carry a portable typewriter. If you rent a typewriter, specify the size type you need, the make, and manual or electric.

Room Arrangement.   At the time you request hotel accommodations, state that "Mr. Bound and secretary" will be occupying whatever type reservations you request. The hotel should then reserve rooms for you and your boss on different floor levels. Upon arrival, should you discover that both your boss' room and your room are on the same floor, politely call this to the attention of those in charge at the hotel so that accommodations can be changed to meet your original request, which means that without requesting different floor levels the hotel should place you on a different floor level from that of your boss.

At the time you call or write for reservations for a future date, you may indicate or direct your request to: "Reservations, Future." If it is necessary for you to contact the hotel about a reservation on the day the room is to be occupied, direct your request to: "Reservations, Present." (In smaller hotels, it may not be necessary to specify time—future or present.)

A Time to Dine.   When your work takes you away from your home office, you probably will keep your regular schedule for breakfast, lunch, and dinner.

An invitation from the business executive to have lunch together may be an exception to your eating schedule. Combining lunch breaks during a trip away from home may save time.

You may ask the waiter or waitress about the food listed on the menu, but place your selection through your escort. Do not experiment with unfamiliar food preparations on this trip. Order whatever you know will agree with you. Your boss cannot afford to have you become ill. Order food for the nutritional value, and try to stay in good health throughout the trip.

Who Leads the Way to the Table?   Many restaurants and tearooms have a head waiter or hostess. In these dining facilities, you follow the head waiter or hostess; the man follows you. If a head waiter or hostess is not on duty, you follow your escort to the table. You would be seated in the chair that faces toward the greater portion of the room. Approach the chair from the left side of it. A man seats a lady first; he then sits in the chair directly across from the lady or to *her left*. (One hostess, in particular, usually touches the chair or pulls it away from the table slightly to signal where the lady is to be seated.)

The lunch break is for sustenance; and although your seating arrangement may not win an etiquette award, good manners and politeness should make the best impression on those who serve you.

To simplify the proper place for you, tell yourself that you are the boss' "right-hand secretary"—you walk and sit to the right of him.

The Tab and Tips.   When you travel together, your boss tips for the two of you.

You do your own tipping for services rendered for you when you are alone on a business trip, but you must keep records of all amounts spent so that the company will reimburse you according to expense account policy.

If your boss invites you to lunch, he no doubt intends to pay. He picks up the tab, leaves the tip; you thank him. He then puts this down on his expense account, if he maintains an expense list.

A Time to Work. The dictation quarters are set aside in your boss' reserved area, but never in the secretary's room.

The away-from-home office should be in order before you report for work. It may be worthwhile to request maid service for the executive's reserved area the night before so that the rooms will be in order by a specified time the following morning.

The Secretary Is a Lady. Secretaries should be "proper." If you do your part by taking the role of a lady, the men can then be gentlemen. Allow them to open doors when the polite gesture is extended to you. Do not insist that you can manage to move a filing cabinet, desk, typewriters, or chairs, if a man offers to move these objects for you.

The executive should be encircled with loyalty and respect. A secretary who is devoted to her business status should not attempt to crush the business image of her boss.

Training Your Successor

Apparently you have accepted and performed your office tasks very well. You have proof now that you were definitely qualified for this job. You've organized your work areas to the point where you have complete control of the work flow.

Your willingness to accept new responsibilities undoubtedly will be recognized by the company. Perhaps you will be promoted to another important job within the company. Or perhaps you will continually test your ability by seeking new challenges on unfamiliar ground.

Whatever your destiny in the business world, beyond your present position, you can help prepare others to meet the responsibilities of your position. A procedures manual can be one of the most helpful tools in an office. If it is necessary that you terminate your employment with the company, a procedures manual can be a guide for your successor. She will then have some knowledge of the methods used to meet the demands of the position.

The Training Program, Step by Step. Plan a training program that will eliminate an abrupt transfer of the office responsibilities. Before the actual training begins, background material (pamphlets, brochures and company literature) should be given to the newcomer. She should learn something about the history and size of the company.

Ask your successor to read your procedures manual, to gain an insight of the steps involved in performing the duties and to

260

envision the scope of your job as it relates to your boss' position and to the entire company.

The official training program begins with Step No. 1, Greet Your Successor.

Step No. 1: Greet Your Successor. Plan to arrive a few minutes earlier than usual and be in your office to greet your successor. Show her where to hang wraps and place her personal items.

Step No. 2: Introduce Her to Others. The first day that your successor reports for work, introduce her to those with whom she will have frequent contact and to those individuals with whom she will be working closely—employees of another department whose work is closely related to the department in which she will work.

Step No. 3: Tour the Premises. Following the introduction session, a tour of the premises would be in order. The tour would cover the area immediately surrounding her work area. Other areas may be pointed out to her, particularly those that are either directly or indirectly related to your work.

Step No. 4: Observation Day. The first day should be designated as Observation Day for your successor. This will give her an idea of the pace required in performing the office tasks, how time is scheduled, and which projects have priority. Throughout the first day, your successor should portray the role of your "shadow."

Step No. 5: Explain Desk Arrangement. Open the desk drawers, one by one; look at every item, *not* to explain *what* the items are *but where* they are. Have your desk well supplied, but take the time to show her where the supplies are stored.

Step No. 6: Explain Filing System. Open the filing cabinet drawers, one at a time, and explain the filing system. Point out the file guides as they correspond with the labels on the front of the filing cabinet drawers.

Step No. 7: Communicate with Your Successor. Explain to your successor every move you make and why you handled a situation in the manner you did. Begin now to let her "in" on the telephone calls, although you may not expect her to answer the telephone the first day.

Step No. 8: File the Correspondence.   You probably have correspondence in your filing tray that is ready to be filed. Turn to the File Directory section of your procedures manual. As you pick up a letter to be filed, explain the contents of it, point out the caption for the proper folder. Make a notation, with pencil, in the upper left-hand corner of the letter where the letter is to be filed. (The pencil notation will be the same as the caption on the respective file folder.) Lay this letter aside and continue this procedure through the remaining papers to be filed.

When this first task is completed, sort the papers for filing, as you alone would do. Both, or either, of you may file the correspondence.

Step No. 9: Explain the Communication System.   Explain to your successor how she is expected to answer the telephone. Give her precise instructions for using the communication instruments for relaying calls to your boss. Before your successor begins answering the telephone, have her read the business telephone directory (described in Chapter 3, "Office Telephone Calls") which you had compiled from messages recorded earlier; pronounce any names in the directory which are unfamiliar to her, and explain the business "connection" between the business firm listed in the business telephone directory that you prepared and your company.

Following this introductory session, your successor may begin answering the telephone, relaying the calls to your boss, and taking messages if your boss is out of the office.

Step No. 10: Listen as Your Successor Greets the Office Visitors.   The next assignment for your successor is to greet the office visitors. Explain any previously scheduled appointments already written on the calendars—who the individual is and the purpose of his visit.

Step No. 11: Turn the Daily Appointment Calendar over to Your Successor.   Tell your successor how much time is usually allotted for specific appointments. For example, an individual scheduled for an interview with your boss may not require the same amount of time as an individual who is scheduled to outline the terms and conditions of a contract. With your help, your successor may schedule appointments for company officials who must confer with your boss and for other employees who are to report to your boss' office at his request.

Step No. 12: Describe "Desk Services" to Her. Tell your successor about the desk services provided for your boss, as they are outlined in Chapter 18. Suggest that she ready his desk and office by herself. You should be there to be sure that she does not overlook any details.

Step No. 13: Describe the Mail and How It Is Handled. This step of the training period involves the mail. Be exact so that your successor will know what is expected of her when the mail must be taken care of. Have her underline the main points in the body of the letter, then show her where she is to obtain the requested information so that the letter can be answered correctly. The various details for handling the mail are described in Chapter 4.

Step No. 14: Prime Your Successor for the Business Trip. Planning the itinerary is the next step in the training process. Your successor must know what your boss expects from his secretary in the way of readying his papers for business trips. Chapter 16 outlines the preparations for the business trips.

Step No. 15: Brief Your Successor on the Social Functions. Brief her on the social functions. Let her know if she will be expected to handle any personal and social details, and in what capacity she might be expected to participate. Be sure she knows what events are scheduled, if any; and whether or not she must devote some of her time to holiday festivities.

Step No. 16: Hand Your Successor the Keys. When the on-the-job training period officially ends, the procedures manual must serve as a replacement for the oral instruction. The procedures manual will be a guide for your successor, whoever she is, when she inherits, through an interview, your keys to the office.

SELECTED BIBLIOGRAPHY

Agnew, Peter L., and James R. Meehan. *Secretarial Office Practice.* 6th edition. South-Western Publishing Company, 1960.

The Art of Business Etiquette, Prentice-Hall Better Secretaries Series. Englewood Cliffs, New Jersey: Prentice-Hall, Inc., 1962.

The Bankers' Handbook. Edited by William H. Baughn and Charls E. Walker. Homewood, Illinois: Dow-Jones-Irwin, Inc., 1966.

Becker, Esther R., and Peggy Norton Rollason. *The High-Paid Secretary.* Englewood Cliffs, New Jersey: Prentice-Hall, Inc., 1967.

Bendixen, Ethel T., and Helen Schneider Ricksen. *Production Typing.* South-Western Publishing Company, 1951. p. 42, 43, 48.

Business Etiquette Handbook. By the Parker Publishing Company Editorial Staff. West Nyack, New York: Parker Publishing Company, Inc., 1965.

Chamberlin, Coleman R. *Filing Facts.* New York: National Filing Aid Bureau, 1953.

Correspondence Manual. Washington, D.C.: United States Government Printing Office, 1968.

Demeter, George. *Demeter's Manual of Parliamentary Law and Procedure.* Blue Book edition. Boston, Massachusetts: Little, Brown and Company, 1969.

Doris, Lillian, and Besse Mae Miller. *Complete Secretary's Handbook.* Englewood Cliffs, New Jersey: Prentice-Hall, Inc., March, 1957.

Funk & Wagnalls Standard Dictionary, International edition. New York: Funk & Wagnalls Company, 1958 and 1959. Volumes One and Two.

Gavin, Ruth E., and Lillian E. Hutchinson. *Reference Manual for Stenographers and Typists.* 3rd edition. New York: McGraw-Hill Book Company, Inc., 1961.

How to Train an Assistant or Substitute. Prentice-Hall Better Secretaries Series. Englewood Cliffs, New Jersey: Prentice-Hall, Inc., 1962.

Kahn, Gilbert, and Theodore Yerian, and Jeffrey R. Stewart, Jr. *Progressive Filing.* 7th edition. New York: McGraw-Hill Book Company, Inc., 1961.

Lessenberry, D. D., and T. James Crawford, and Lawrence W. Erickson. *20th Century Typewriting.* 7th edition. New York: South-Western Publishing Company, 1957.

Lloyd, Alan C., and Russell J. Hasler. *Personal Typing.* 3rd edition. Gregg Division, McGraw-Hill Book Company, 1969.

A Manual of Style. 12th edition. Chicago: The University of Chicago Press, 1969.

McCrimmon, James M. *Writing with a Purpose.* 4th edition. New York: Houghton Mifflin Co., 1967, p 370-380.

Office Short Cuts and Time Savers. Prentice-Hall Better Secretaries Series. Englewood Cliffs, New Jersey: Prentice-Hall, Inc., 1962.

Official Catholic Directory, Edited by Thomas B. Kenedy. New York: P. J. Kenedy & Sons, 1968, page x.

Parkhurst, Charles Chandler. *English for Business.* 4th edition. Englewood Cliffs, New Jersey: Prentice-Hall, 1963.

Saving Time and Money on Mail and Telegrams. Prentice-Hall Better Secretaries Series. Englewood Cliffs, New Jersey: Prentice-Hall, Inc., 1962.

Smart, Walter Kay. *English Review Grammar.* 4th edition. New York: Appleton-Century-Crofts, Inc., 1959.

Taintor, Sarah Augusta, and Kate M. Monro. *Secretary's Handbook.* 8th edition revised. New York: The Macmillan Company, November, 1967.

Webster's Seventh New Collegiate Dictionary. Springfield, Massachusetts: G. & C. Merriam Company, 1963.

The World Book Atlas, 1969 edition, Chicago: Field Enterprises Educational Corporation, p. 165.

The World Book Encyclopedia, U.S.A.: Field Enterprises Educational Corporation, Volume 19, 1965, pp. 63 and 75.

Index

A

Abbreviations:
  capital letters and no periods,
    127
  firm names, 126-127
  forming plurals of, 105
  two-letter of States, 101
  using period with, 111
Absentee ballot, 251
Acknowledging the mail, 51-52
Additions and corrections in mail-
    ing list, 235
Address:
  complete, 96
  four or more lines, 77-78
  incorrect, 41-42
  models of written:
    academic, 79
    business, 80
    ecclesiastical, 80-81
    governmental, 82-83
    professional, 83-84
  the spoken, 23-24
  three-line, 77-78
Addressograph-Multigraph Corpora-
    tion, 165
Agenda, 210, 214
Air Mail, 95, 96, 102
Air travel cards, 216

Alphabetical Directory, numeric
    filing system, used with,
    192-194
Alphabetical filing, 183-184
American Telephone and Telegraph
    Company, 40
Annual reminders, 251
Answering mail, 43-55
Answering telephone, 35-37
Apostrophe:
  to form contractions, 105
  to form plural of abbreviations,
    105
  to indicate minutes, 105
  to indicate omissions, 105
  to show possession (Ownership),
    104-105
  with letters, 105
Application letters, handling, 44
Appointments:
  canceling, 34
  color scheme for listing, 32-33
  confirming, 31, 37
  for personal interview, 44
  listing daily, 32
  maintaining day's schedule of,
    32
  marking calendar, 32
Appointments, schedule of, for
    business trip, 215

Y

Youth Dew Cologne, 257

Z

ZIP Code, 77, 96, 101
Zoning Improvement Plan (*see* ZIP
    Code)